Love and Money,
Sex and Death

Love and Money, Sex and Death

A Memoir

McKenzie Wark

VERSO

London • New York

First published by Verso 2023
© McKenzie Wark 2023

1 3 5 7 9 10 8 6 4 2

Verso
UK: 6 Meard Street, London W1F 0EG
US: 388 Atlantic Avenue, Brooklyn, NY 11217
versobooks.com

Verso is the imprint of New Left Books

ISBN-13: 978-1-80429-261-7
ISBN-13: 978-1-80429-262-4 (UK EBK)
ISBN-13: 978-1-80429-263-1 (US EBK)

British Library Cataloguing in Publication Data
A catalogue record for this book is available from the British Library

Library of Congress Cataloging-in-Publication Data

Names: Wark, McKenzie, 1961– author.
Title: Love and money, sex and death : a memoir / McKenzie Wark.
Description: London ; New York : Verso Books, 2023.
Identifiers: LCCN 2023016693 (print) | LCCN 2023016694 (ebook) | ISBN
  9781804292617 (hardback) | ISBN 9781804292631 (ebk)
Subjects: LCSH: Wark, McKenzie, 1961– | Transgender
  women—Australia—Biography. | Transgender college teachers—United
  States—Biography.
Classification: LCC HQ77.8.W36 A3 2023 (print) | LCC HQ77.8.W36 (ebook) |
  DDC 306.76/8092 [B]—dc23/eng/20230515
LC record available at https://lccn.loc.gov/2023016693
LC ebook record available at https://lccn.loc.gov/2023016694

Typeset in Sabon by MJ & N Gavan, Truro, Cornwall
Printed and bound by CPI Group (UK) Ltd, Croydon CR0 4YY

One's real life is so often the life that one does not lead.
Oscar Wilde

Contents

0.1

(To McKenzie)

When Little Richard came to our hometown, he left us something like a gift. He came to Newcastle on his Australian tour, in 1957, four years before you were born. He was this churning, surging flame, icon of a new thing called rock and roll. Then his life took a turn while crossing the waters of our harbor.

Your life will take some turns too. I'm writing this to you from your own future, or a possible one at least. A letter to a young poet, where the young poet is me, forty years ago, not quite twenty years old. A letter that's cover for a medley of others, addressed to others, about love and money, sex and death.

You—what do I even remember of you? Our past selves are probably extensively edited editions. Let me see what I can piece together.

I'll try not to advise, as you won't take advice. You never seek it. You are incapable of being mentored. A lot of people will help you. Perhaps they see the wound that keeps you from asking. They'll help you in spite of your indifference, even antagonism, to care. To accepting love.

You don't think about this much, but I have to insist: we lost our mother young, and we never much liked our distant, irritable father. The two frontline adults meant to be there for us, keep the world at bay, weren't. That made us distrustful, detached, dissociated. Look that last one up, it explains a lot. Like in *Kimba the White Lion*, that TV show you loved when you were little, you feel alone in the world.

It is obvious to you already that a world that relies on little isolated family units subject to the whims of the market and disease is a bad idea. You want a better world. The past hurt you, so you move on, and want the world to move on. You've not yet learned to live in the present, so you live in the nothingness of a permanent not-yet.

Your family tended their own wounds after your mother died. As the youngest, you couldn't see that. You needed them all to not fall apart so they could hold you together. They did their best, but you needed more than that, so you started looking for ways to get attention.

Big brother smoked. You found an old cigarette tin, rolled pencil stubs in paper, and made them into a fake brand. You called them "Snazzies: the cigarette for the fancy smoker." You made it into a bit, and everyone thought it was cute. Bigger kids still pushed you up against a wall and took things from you, but sometimes they too could be charmed.

You feel vulnerable, fragile, too open to the randomness of the world. You've already got good at monitoring the perimeter, scanning for danger, checking you have all your kit. You've just moved to Sydney from your hometown, and those skills come in handy.

Don't think I've forgotten that time you came back to Newcastle and slept on a former schoolmate's couch rather than go visit your father. Don't think I've forgotten how, hard up for cash, you sold a matchbox of weed to someone else you thought you'd left behind. He complained it wasn't much pot for five bucks. You said take it or leave it. He took it, but got his bigger mates to find you, sit you in a car and make you roll the regulation five joints out of it under threat of consequences. And you did. Grace under pressure. And all forgotten. Mates again, smoking together in the car. Fuck those losers. You're not living in their world again, ever.

Little Richard left Macon, Georgia, for a life on the road, performing. He was the son of a preacher who also owned a nightclub. He grew up religious. What he loved most was the ecstatic, stirring energy of church. The intensity of it, that raving joy and surrender in a racist world of pain, poverty, and police. Not like your upbringing at all, although there might be one thing you have in common.

Now back home for another brief visit in Newcastle, back to that steel, coal and port town with its belching smoke and bending beaches. You were right to fuck off immediately after high school. You need a city big enough to let you get weird. You want your life to be Wildean and singular. Mate, you have no idea.

You won't listen, but I want to talk to you anyway. Need to, perhaps. Need to make contact in some way with that skinny teenage boy. Boy? Man? That's the rub. Or part of it. You take refuge in androgyny. That picture of Patti Smith on the cover of *Horses* is your icon. Your hair long, wearing girls' jeans, girls' boots. With your slight frame, you're often mistaken for a girl, and you like it. Whatever those situations point toward, you're avoiding. Diverting elsewhere with ambitions, politics, writing, some less happy pursuits.

The thing about diversions is that you can never see what's coming up around the turn.

The diversions will go on a long time. Probably too long. What if you stopped diverting yourself? Or rather, diverted yourself differently? Imagine there's streams of parallel time-lines, alternate ones, in which you come out as trans at forty, or thirty, or—right now. In some of those timelines, I'm not here in your future to be writing you. In this one, we kept ourselves safe, biding our time till we could come out and remain alive.

Little Richard had to get out, so he invented rock and roll. The driving beat, the thriving bass, the ecstatic merge. A church-like joy without sacrifice. He performed in drag sometimes, as Princess Lavonne. He—or she—was so different to you but in this maybe a little bit the same. Like you, she loved women whom she wanted to be. She was a girl, and maybe on some level knew it. The only way out was a detour into rock and roll, her art.

You already suspect it—your poetry is bad. Give it up. You're a prose writer. You're just too lazy to fill the whole page. You read mainly prose anyway, a lot of it, from your late mother's library. Lots of cheap Penguin paperbacks of modernist master-pieces. You read moderns to become modern. A whole social democratic education across the yellowing, flaking pages, as if you were in a race to read them before the acid eats the paper.

You have access to a charge account at Ell's bookstore, although sometimes you steal from it anyway, but that's another story. Science fiction holds your attention when it creates that modern feeling of estrangement from what the reader expects. Much of what you read is bad, but there's something about reading your way out of this world into another that fills a need.

School was mostly a bore, so you read on your own. Your other source of books, and more, is the local branch of the Communist Party of Australia. The comrades: our marvelous mentors. I still know how to run efficient meetings. Your communism, like more things than you care to know, is more felt than thought. About your mother's suffering, you could do nothing; about the suffering of labor, that need not be as inevitable as death.

Little Richard was on tour in Australia when the Soviet sat-ellite *Sputnik* arced bright overhead. An aluminum orb, trailing techno beeps on shortwave radio. That read like an omen, a portent. It was calling. Something had to be sacrificed in a cold world war whose looming strife seemed of biblical proportions. And that offering would be made, by Little Richard, right there in the town where you were born.

In the district party office hung two portraits, Marx flanked by Lenin, strung on two of three nails. On the third, bare, once hung Stalin. Opposite: a vivid poster of comrade Angela Davis. Like in a chapel, she is in the place of the mother, facing off against the father, son, and holy ghost. One had come down from his nail already.

When Soviet tanks churned into Czechoslovakia in 1968, the party split, as elsewhere, into tank and anti-tank factions. On this rare occasion, the anti-tankies, those who denounced the Russians for invading another socialist state, prevailed. The party became a mix of old left and new left, obliged to get along by the rules of democratic centralism.

The comrades remained in solidarity with the revolution even though they knew, in their gut, that we are a defeated people, a lost cause. Yet at least they refused to concede, to acquiesce. Which was maybe why it was the comrades alone whom you accepted as elders. And why I still hold them in my heart, still write to pass along their endless struggle to come.

When the Soviet Union invaded Afghanistan in 1979, the local party elders entrusted you to lead the discussion at the branch meeting. You affirmed the party line, condemning it. Opening up an old wound for those who remembered when Soviet tanks rolled into Prague, or before that Budapest.

You had heard about the invasion via car radio, driving at night on a dark country lane heading back to Sydney from your sister's place in the country. After the news flash, the car died. Just stopped running, and on a blind curve. Electrics dead. Looking at the bright light on the horizon, your first thought was: well, that's it then. Nuclear war. Sydney's gone. The car's electrics fried by the electromagnetic pulse. You sat with that thought for a bit. Then questioned it. The flashlight still worked, so you got out and looked under the hood. A cable had come off the battery.

You became the repository of many stories. The comrades bore the scars of a series of defeats, some world historical: the Spanish Civil War, Stalinism, the Sino-Soviet split, the massacre of the party and many others in Indonesia, the failure of the new left, the coups against Nkrumah in Ghana, Allende in Chile. Some more local, such as the party's failed attempt at a general strike in 1948, and the loss of some of its considerable power in the union movement in the cold war decades. You felt these personally.

You also heard tell of more local struggles. How the coastal shipping was unionized—after lights out, with fists. How the party fought evictions in the depression by destroying the property the bailiffs came to claim. Or how Bob Hawke, a future prime minister, drunk as a skunk, pissed under the table at a May Day function in the Namatjira Room of the Newcastle Workers' Club.

You divert yourself from yourself with politics, but then the diversion within the diversion, of political art. A predictable turn for a petit bourgeois rebel like you. A chance encounter with Maurice Nadeau's *History of Surrealism* laid out a key moment in the tension between political and aesthetic revolution. You go looking for that confluence.

You were the first from your high school to find the punk rock scene at the Grand Hotel on Church Street, same street as your father's architecture practice. There was only one good band—Pel Mel, who played every weekend. Some of their songs are still in me.

It is in the space between the political and aesthetic radicals of our old hometown that you met Glenn Hennessy. Just a couple of years older, he wants to fuck you and you know it. But he also cares about you, takes you seriously as someone who reads, who thinks. He makes you meals for the conversation. Glenn is both gay and Aboriginal and is opening up your awareness to both those worlds a little. Please do better to treasure him.

"Am I gay?" I know you ask yourself. Sure, some people just are, but for others, for you, the self can be a lot of things, and can change. Maybe there really is nothing but fiction and property holding the self together through time.

I know you will understand that last sentence. You have already read enough Marx to see how property shapes and sorts everything. You're teaching yourself French by translating

Rimbaud and have puzzled out the phrase "Je est un autre" as "I is an-other," selving as othering. Together through the decades we will vary, elaborate and amplify these discoveries. It's just fiction and property that bound the self and bind it to a line through time.

But if that isn't true, could we even know it?

Anyway, Glenn isn't the first or last man who will want to fuck you. You know you're vulnerable to that attention, which is sometimes benign and sometimes not. You need to feel seen, feel held. You also need to feel feminine. There are ways that this need is exploitable, and you won't always know how to get what you need from these transactions.

I'm not going to say you are a girl, or that you always were. You've been reading transsexual memoirs on the sly already and not finding yourself in that "born in the wrong body" story. You feel like your body is already a girl's body. Sure, you envy the bodies of other girls, the curve of hip and tit, but lots of girls have feelings like that. You feel like it's your self that's too male, not your body. The properties that bind include gender.

Maybe some sorts of transsexual people "always knew," but you didn't. You're always swerving, blindly falling through gender.

For a long time, I "forgot" about this story. I wonder if you've already pushed it out of memory:

The first trans women you met were streetwalkers. Or so you assumed. What did you see when you saw them? When you were nineteen you discovered, by accident, Premier Lane. It's one of those mystery streets of Sydney. The city ambience you love. Dark and narrow and with no obvious reason to exist. Some eighteenth-century colonial surveyor's folly. You have been in Sydney about a year. You are going to Macquarie University on the boring north shore, so you drive over the Sydney Harbour Bridge to the east side for fun. It can be hard to park a car, so you look for those secret spots. That's how you stumble on Premier Lane, the trans sex worker stroll.

7

You'd been dancing in Darlinghurst. Came back to fetch the car and found three girls sitting on top of it, two on the roof and one on the hood, singing along to a transistor radio. "She's got—Bette Davis eyes!" They leaped off quickly, apologized. You told them you didn't mind. They stood their ground though. With a steady gaze, they read you. The trio all rocked the same look. Long hair, short skirts, red lips, fishnets. Wiry, thin, boisterous. About your age. The frames of their bodies so like yours. Speedy: you know from speed already. Talk all jitter-chatter. Big hollow eyes, wide and dark to swallow all light. You've left me no clear image of any of them in memory as their talk cut and wove between kinetic bodies, dancing and singing. "Bette Davis eyes!" Teetering heels on the steepish rake of the lane. They ask you if you want to party. You decline.

They make you anxious, on layered levels. They see your sort. They expose your own contradictions, inhibitions, prejudices. About sexuality, about sex work, about class, about gender, about your inability to think at all about who you might be or who we might become. All the things you find so many ways, useful and not, to avoid thinking and feeling. You feel seen, but also like a voyeur whose glance alights by accident on that scene that looks back at you.

You will become me when it seems like you can—and not die. If you are in receipt of this letter—we made it.

Maybe I shouldn't tell you anything. Maybe it's just random, how we get through time. Or maybe it's like a jazz solo—points chanced through harmonic space, picked out by the player from all the possible others. We love the small-group jazz of Miles, Monk and Coltrane. Jazz is an adventure of connecting one moment to another. (Time is an-other). I know jazz is already a guide for you. Since you not only left Newcastle for Sydney but dream of leaving Sydney for New York, jazz—all of Black music—is a good way to learn the secret history of America.

Let's say no more of what happens, in the drifts and riffs between the times of you and of me. Who even knows if memory is any more reliable than anticipation? The mistakes we made only multiply. They are all we have. And they lead you to become me. Our mistakes are us, you and me. But you are going to hurt Mu. There's nothing I can do to stop that. It's one of the few things we will regret while we breathe.

Little Richard heard the call in Newcastle. Some say this happened in Sydney, some say Newcastle, which for our purposes is a more interesting story. On the waters of the harbor, on the ferry—the punt as we used to call it. She thought the call came from God. And maybe it did, or maybe from another deity. She told her bandmates God was calling, right there on the punt, on the water, calling her to change her ways. They said if she is serious that she should cast her precious diamonds and pearls into the waters. And she did.

◆

I keep saying that you won't want to listen to me—but can I listen to you? I'm trying. Older people can lose track of what was vital in our younger selves. That sound of surprise, shock and delight in life. Everything of note sounding out clear, not bound in worn chords of memory. I see my peers hide out in nostalgia. Seeing the same old bands, gone slack, bald and bored.

You aren't bored with life, and neither am I. Honestly, if one has a capacious relation to one's various genders, one could transition just to save oneself from boredom. To be restored to curiosity, even to unpleasant surprises. Changing sex edits your relation to a lot of things. Including history.

Since I transitioned, I've recovered some of your electricity, that lust for life from which you were then also too often detached. From which you divert yourself, with various ambitions, personal, aesthetic, political. I'm trying to bring that into this writing. I'm trying to listen for you, still in me. As you'll see from these other letters, I'm trying to wind back through the wounds. The writing writes us. Writing is the birth of the author; the text is the afterbirth.

Little Richard lost her rings. Later she'd joke that down-under fish have them. I have them now. Well, metaphorically, at least. The sparkle of one's difference. The thing I wandered off in search of, in a manner of speaking, was right here, in the waters of home.

Modems

Mothers

1.1

(To Joyce)

When asked why I write all the time, I never know what to say. I'm back home in Australia, on a flying visit from New York. I want to write to you of the color of the leaves, the birdsong, all we once shared, all tugging at senses, bringing me back to our past, all becoming nebulous, fantastic as the years in New York pile on.

My sister takes me to the storage unit that holds some lost chunk of my Australian and pretransition life. There's the metal shelves I spent two days assembling. There's the double rows of books, slightly random, abandoned and sad.

I'm sorting through it all for the few more personal things I might still care about. Here's that old metal tin. In it, letters from former lovers. I leaf through them, glance at the hand-writing. I know they all complain about the same thing. That the writer cannot reach me, that I remain hidden from them. I was hidden from myself. It gives me no satisfaction to know this now.

Among the letters, a postcard. A picture of an institutional building. Somehow, I know it's a hospital. I turn the card over. It is your handwriting, Mum. You are writing to me from this hospital. The last place you were ever to be.

I smash-cut into a memory of visiting you there. I'm with my father, your husband, on the long drive from Newcastle down the old Pacific Highway to Sydney. I am six years old. The ride bores me. We pass the exit sign for Crows Nest. Funny name for a place, I say. Dad asks me to be quiet. He is trying not to get lost.

I've brought something to show you in the hospital. A paper cone, colored in with pencils. There's a flat paper head attached. She is a princess. Maybe I made her at Sunday school. We are not a religious family. It felt like I was sent across the road to the Baptist Sunday school to get me out of the house. Give my father and older siblings a break. I'm holding my paper princess. I see that my coloring is not quite as good as I'd like. The blush color of her face has a flaw. I missed a bit. But I don't have my pencils to fix it.

I show you. The feeling that remains, from this moment, long ago, is one of disappointment. Your reaction wasn't anything. I can now put myself in your place, but I don't let myself dwell on what you could have felt, to see your youngest child, a little grumpy from the car ride, chattering away, as if nothing was happening, while knowing that this child might soon be motherless. I am older now than you were then. I have kids of my own. If I think about this too much, your pain becomes mine. Almost.

There is none of this in your postcard. Its tone is light, written to a child, in your loopy hand. This memory from the hospital is one of exactly nine memories I have of you. I ask my sister, Sue, to tell me a bit about you as I remember so little. My sister says that Joyce Wark was brave and proud and reserved. You didn't let your feelings show. You went out of this life keeping your suffering to yourself.

The thing I know best about you is your taste in literature. Your books filled our house, long after you were gone. I spent a week putting them into alphabetical order. My father gave a brace of your hardbacks away once, and I was furious with him, although I did not know why. I think now that the books were my link to you. I read them to find you. You appreciated literary modernism. I contracted that taste from those yellowing pages. You even had Joyce's *Ulysses*, which was banned in Australia for a time.

Another of my handful of memories of you: a time you took

me to the Cardiff public library. We are in the children's section. It was after play school, where you took me one morning a week. I liked it there. I liked the two little girls I played with, but they never invited me to their special tea party under the slippery dip. Until one day, they did. Taste of weak tea in a little cup. It started to rain. We were all called inside. I was sad because I did not get to play their tea party game.

Maybe you took me to the library to cheer me up that day. I remember you as a warm presence, a benign ambience, but I don't have an image of you. All I remember of the library is the bright colors of the books, in rows, in racks, primary reds, yellows, blues. Some exotic-looking books in purple and orange. I had to choose just one book, but I wanted them all.

Writing is what you gave me, what left traces. You must have given me other things. You loved me. I feel that this has to be true. I have no way of knowing other than the evidence of my body, my life—that I can love. Since I lost you, letting myself be loved is harder. I've not loved much of myself, either.

Becoming a writer filled the solitude left by your leaving. I know that you did not really abandon me. You had cancer. Feelings don't answer to facts or reason. Sometimes they just make a void around themselves and remain, undetected.

When I started transition and went on hormones, the past all came back to me, came out of its nothingness. All the loss, all the longing, all the pain, and with it an understanding of this compulsion to write, this refuge in writing. When I am writing, I am always writing to you. I am always writing to my mother, to this absence you left in me.

Another memory: we're on a big bed together, and you just read me that Winnie the Pooh story where he attaches himself to a balloon and floats up to steal honey from the bees. They don't fall for it, and Piglet has to get Christopher Robin to come and shoot him down.

You read me that story. I remember this because I read the same story to my own child and the pictures brought it teeming back. I didn't like the story. I didn't like the ending, so I made you tell it a different way. And the balloon had to be orange—my favorite color. I could not read yet, and my minor motor skills were so poor I could not color within the lines—but in that moment, I became a writer.

For fifty-odd years I've been answering your postcard. Telling you about the books I read and how they could go differently. And, finally, I had to write to you about how I was an-other. I had to come out as transsexual not just to the world, but in writing—to you.

Only now I've lost you twice. You weren't there for the child-hood where everyone thought I was a boy and even I believed it, sometimes. And now you are not there for the childhood that I did not have, as a girl. The letters that you are not there to receive are from someone else who you are not there to not recognize. But I keep sending them, as I always have. As I need to do.

For thirty years I've written into the void using the name McKenzie Wark. I never really knew why. McKenzie was the maiden name of your mother, my maternal grandmother. I feel certain now that of my two given names, Kenneth McKenzie, it's the one you chose. Maybe I use McKenzie as a signal, or sigil, flung across blank forgetting so you would know it is me and that I need you. Need you at least to have been.

◆

How could I forget this? I forgot, and forgot to tell you: I started writing, really writing, on what had once been your typewriter. I loved your typewriter, a sleek and modern portable, with its light-gray anodized case. A thing that fit in my childhood home like it belonged among the other modern things. I wrote poems on it, and, of course, a poetry manifesto.

I have no memory of you ever using it. Maybe you had to give up all that when you got married. My sister showed me your psychology degree, and some documents about jobs you had during and just after the war. There's a reference written for you for a job in which some nong of a former boss praised the quality of your typing, and your extensive and "unusual" taste in literature. This was before you became a postwar "homemaker." Not that there was much choice about that in those days.

In your absence I developed a curiosity about the home you made. What parts of it were you and what parts of it were dad? Aesthetically, I mean. It seemed like your tastes were both modern, but were they the same? The square lines of the Baird television. The Snelling chairs, with their repurposed parachute webbing, left over from the war. Whose choice were they? The ornate crystal sherry decanter looked out of place, a throwback to some other model of the middle-class home to our modest modern one.

This was the home that Ross Kenneth Wark, your husband, my father, the architect, designed. What was it like for you, marrying this man, moving from your home in Sydney up to Newcastle, starting a shared life? It's hard for me to imagine your love for him. As I now know from the other side, the amorous life of parents is inconceivable to a child.

I grew apart from him, and I didn't have your hand to hold on to as a guide to life. The conversation I'd started with you as a garrulous child ended. It continued as a dialogue in my head, as I grew quiet, withdrawn. I was told I was "shy." I took a quiet, solitary interest in this household of things. Your piano, gathering dust in the basement, untuned.

All I can know of you and him as a couple comes from memories of material traces from the life you made together. Your books on his built-in shelves. The house itself expressed the sharp lines of his personality. From him I learned a modernism I sense was different to yours. He believed that things could be made better by being better made. Sitting in his lap as he showed me picture books of modern architecture. Which left such an imprint that when I finally saw Frank Lloyd Wright's Fallingwater, I wept.

◆

The thing about becoming a transsexual is that most of us can't draw on much of a transsexual culture. We have to sort out ways to be by cutting and pasting from the cultural materials that are around us. Which is not what we were supposed to make of those things. We're not who we were expected to become.

I'm not anyone you thought would ever be who your child became. I feel like I have to account for how all that came to pass. How I both continued in the slipstream of the modern house, that he designed, that you made our home, that was your life—and diverted it.

I learned modernism indirectly, from living within that house on Main Road, Cardiff Heights. Just outside of Newcastle. A tiny, open-plan, flat-roofed weatherboard box nested snug into the side of a steep ravine, with views across the valley below, to Lake Macquarie beyond. It's still there, seventy-five years later, much modified, still hidden in green.

From his house itself I learned an aesthetic. One pared of any excrescence. One where form was all. Where anything that wasn't form was meant to reveal it. This was design through subtraction. That was what made it modern. Aesthetics was a practice of extraction, from all that seemed unnecessary, out-dated, mystified, raw. What it would take to get to the future was a severing of much that bound us to the past.

Not too long before he passed, Ross and I had lunch together in a big new hotel in the coastal town of Terrigal. That hotel sat on the site of the Florida Hotel that he designed. It was the first big commission for his practice, Mayo & Wark. It was famous as the venue where for many years the state branch of the Labor Party held its annual conference.

When I had lunch with him, it was gone, replaced by this bigger one, owned by some Japanese hotel chain. I asked him how it felt that the Florida, his first big job, was gone and replaced. He paused, then said with a shrug: "It's progress." Now *that* is modernism. Unsentimental. Forward-facing. Best not to think too much about the past.

Did he forget you? I doubt it. But he did forget to tell me much about you. When I was sixteen, I was distracting myself from a masculine puberty about which I was not particularly thrilled by spending a good deal of time with books and bicycles. One evening, as I sat in contemplation of the clean, efficient lines of the racing bike I was building, Ross came in and said: "It was ten years ago today that your mother died. She would have been proud of you." Then left the room. That was it. The only time I can remember when he spoke of you. That, too, is modernism. The spare use of the past, as there to build on, move forward, roll along.

Ours was a provincial, colonial modernism. Its internal contradictions became clearer to me after I left Australia. My paternal ancestors had been in Australia for a long time by colonial standards, which is to say, not long at all. They came as gasworks engineers. They were quite literally gaslighters. They acted like only darkness preceded them. There's a direct line from that indifference to the past to his, and to mine.

Because I had to get away from him, I took an interest in what he could not abide. What that apostle of high modernism Adolf Loos called "ornament and crime." All that the modern desire for order as progress excluded caught my attention. All of its bad others, those that universal progress demanded get in line or be pushed aside. All those marked by too much Blackness, queerness, femininity, or just by the pleasures of the moment. Or those whose desire for revolution was, let's just say, not entirely constructive.

I don't think you would have been proud of me if you'd known what I got up to without him knowing.

I tried to get out of the sort of modernism that Ross embodied and enacted by reversing it. If, for modernism, form was true and appearance was not, then this metaphysics could be turned inside out. Treat the appearances as real, the inner essence or ideal as an illusion. This was postmodern aesthetics as Oedipal break-up. The joke was on me. To become postmodern was to repeat the modern gesture in a way one's more open-minded modern ancestors might even recognize. There really is nothing else for someone like me. There's no past, no arcadia. But no future either. Maybe there's only sideways time for those of us born of the gaslighters of history.

◆

To be modern is to try to live without superstition, but then how to account for the time I saw your ghost? I was eighteen. Done with school. About to go off to Sydney and university. Deeply depressed, I now recognize, for the only time in my life. Sleeping all day. Waking up on the sofa with a start from a nightmare. Panic, disorientation, loneliness, fear. That's when I sensed your presence, looking down on me, with compassion, with love, and I felt like I could go on.

My modern self doesn't believe in ghosts. My modern self might think I took comfort from the material traces you'd left around me. You weren't there, but certain objects, media arti-facts, were left behind as clues, as evidence, of how you lived your life, and how I might live mine. Art, like writing, came mediated through you. A thing I learned when I became a parent too: that to your kids you are—among other things—media.

I was a child of the mass media age, of mechanical repro-duction. Thousands had these same artifacts. But for me they all had the aura of home, were part of it, part of the world and part of you at the same time. I became a spy in the house of your absence, in the home you'd made.

The first clue I spied to another sensibility was a big picture book about the Acropolis. In the architectural drawings, the clean lines of classical form; in the photos, the scars of time, dirt, disintegration. And, most shocking of all, images that imagined from the leftover flecks what it all would have looked like painted in the gaudy colors the Greeks actually liked. A clue to the other side of what was supposed to be a modern inheritance. That even the Greeks were about something other than order, unity, form—and whiteness.

Snooping around the bookshelves, I found a series of small paperback books with color plates about artists. Were these the ones you most liked? René Magritte, Raoul Dufy, Joan Miró, Paul Klee. They connect to a vague memory of being in the kitchen with you, painting in watercolors. Orange on the off-white of butcher's paper. The lines unfurl in these books, break out of straightness, take on color and feeling.

The jazz records in the house were big band swing—Count Basie, Duke Ellington. I thought them old hat, but I investigated them anyway. From jazz, I learned something about ornament that is compatible with restraint. To hear the silence as part of the music. There's no essence to extract. Form emerges out of details flirting together.

It's telling that I learned about Andy Warhol from "the box," as we called television. Of all the glimpses of the other side of the modern, its color and glamour and ornament and play, its appearances and passing situations, Warhol was the one that pointed to the kind of otherness within and against the modern to which I might one day belong: to transsexuality.

More than Warhol, it was the Factory that intrigued me. And in particular, Candy Darling. Of Warhol's three trans goddesses, she was the prettiest one. I don't know when her image beamed into my world, but I loved her from the start. A book of Richard Avedon pictures I stole as a teen has a group portrait of Warhol Factory regulars, including Candy. Her naked body, tits and dick, transfixed me.

Transsexuality is technically modern, but I'm starting to feel like it's something ancient as well. Maybe there's no essence to the sexed body. Flesh is always-other. It can be diverted, elaborated, ornamented, in different directions, although not without a certain effort. We cut and fold flesh. Like text, like collage.

You taught me something about all this, about form, through your own art. I don't imagine you had much time for art, pressed into the mold of a postwar homemaker. I don't imagine you had much time of your own at all. You liked to arrange flowers. Ikebana, the Japanese art of flowers, was popular in the sixties. You had a book about it. I remember the scent of cut stems. Your secateurs, which I was not allowed to touch. The various vases.

I watched as you made such pretty things, out of these few elements, and put them out to see. Bright and shapely against the cool, hard lines around. There for a few days, then gone. If I could just be that. Be a flower you put, just so, held so gently in your hands. Or even just a simple paper princess. Adorning along with all that adorns, that is the world. That would be enough.

My big sister, Sue, says you were "broad-minded." But I have held the hands and wiped the tears for many transsexuals whose parents had been so too. Sometimes gender is stronger than love. If you'd lived, if I'd come out to you—in my cut and folded form—would you have still loved me? I can't know. Don't want to know.

1.2

(To Joyce)

There are photos of you helping me learn to walk. Mother and child, where the child has plaster casts on both legs. I'd been told I first walked in the casts as a family story, but somehow seeing the photographic evidence makes it something else.

The pictures are on a thumb drive my brother gave me of some old family photos that he transferred from mildewed slides. I don't know what's memory and what's media, especially when it comes to you. So I'm writing to you again.

When one transitions to another sex, the past comes back as if in a different medium. Memories tell not of who one was but who one wasn't. I was who I wasn't for the longest time. Transition brings rushes of the past back. Shots for an incomplete home movie. I had to edit memory as I edited flesh. It goes something like this now.

When I was small, I liked make-believe games. I remember being naked in my room, acting out superhero characters I made up, like the ones in those Japanese cartoons on television. Props were whatever objects were to hand. I took a child's plastic bow and put it around my waist, the string at the back, the bow like invisible wings, curved around the belly. With a cartoon flash that went right through flesh, I became Bow Girl. Then she took the bow from her body and pretended that it hadn't happened. And kept on pretending, for the longest time.

Fifty-odd years later, when I started transition and the edit of the movie of my life fell apart, a lot of scenes got cut, but two stuck. In an otherwise uneventful childhood, they stick out. Always did. But what they have to do with this story now—that

is the puzzle. Both are bad things that happened. I'll start with the second worst.

The second-worst thing that happened when I was little, about age six, was that my father took me on his knee and told me that you were dead. It was a very different sort of flash that went through me. Not one where I became someone else. One where I became nothing at all. That was the second-worst thing I remember.

The worst was a different sort of moment. I hadn't thought about it for the longest time. In the scale of things that can happen to a child, it isn't all that bad. Except to me. And since I'm saying to you, of all people, that the loss of a child's mother is the second-worst thing in that child's life—this calls for some explanation.

Not long after you died, I was in Royal Newcastle Hospital. In those days the hospital was right on Newcastle Beach. Sometimes you could hear the waves. I was in the children's ward. As you know, I was born with clubbed feet. Both feet turned inward and pointed downward. I'd had an operation on them as an infant. This is what is in those photos my brother gave me: it's me, learning to walk with casts on both legs, and you helping. I don't look terribly happy about it. More like some grim determination to become bipedal.

There were various other attempts to fix these feet. I was strapped into a contraption every night, feet forced to point outward. My father tried to save money by making the thing out of a toy Meccano building kit, but the nuts and bolts kept coming lose, and tore the sheets. He had to spring for the surgical appliance—and new sheets.

The foot brace was a torment. Lying on my back, I couldn't close my eyes to fall asleep. I still can't. I lay awake looking at the darkness. My room was very dark. I liked the swirling patterns the almost-blackness made if I kept my eyes open. Everything visible could dissolve and swirl. Images emerged out of the patterns, and out of the images, stories.

The best but scariest story on television was the science fiction serial *Doctor Who*. Its tape-loop theme music was a portal to a dimension bigger than the box on which the show played. The most terrifying villains on *Doctor Who* were the alien robot Daleks. I find it hard to believe how scary they seemed to me then.

When my oldest child and I visited the Doctor Who Museum in London, not long ago, they had some of the actual Daleks used on the show. The docent took our picture with them. We were supposed to pose as if shooting them with lasers, but I didn't want to shoot them. The Daleks looked so vulnerable. Just bits of plywood, cardboard, and glue.

When I was little, one of my favorite stories to tell myself while trying to get to sleep was about Daleks. I am tied up in a blank room. I must go to sleep. If I do not sleep, the Daleks will exterminate me. (It's what they do.) The Daleks come into the room over and over to check on me. I pretend to be asleep. Except there is one Dalek who is not like the others and who is my friend. This one is orange. I don't know where the color came from, as our TV was black and white. This Dalek knows and accepts that I go to sleep with my eyes open, making ornamenting patterns out of the invisible world.

I had another round of operations on my feet around the age of seven. I was in the public ward. They did one foot, then the other. The first time it was all a bit disorienting. A night in the hospital. A mysterious sign over my bed that read "Nil by Mouth." The next morning, hungry. Wheeled on a gurney about the hospital, which seemed an endless maze. Nurses in white uniforms and white hats. That antiseptic smell. The big black rubber mask coming down over my face. The smell of the gas that put me under, while I counted. The second before losing consciousness, not wanting to go. I imagine this is what it is like to die.

I woke up not knowing where I was. I was not back on the ward but in some crepuscular space, where maybe I wasn't supposed to be awake. Or maybe I awoke in the wrong world. I closed my eyes and pretended I wasn't. Eventually, they wheeled me back to the ward. Where my right leg was supposed to be was some uncanny sensation. Like it wasn't there but something else was. It was supposed to be a better version of my foot, but it felt like a giant claw that I could touch on the outside but not feel on the inside.

That afternoon wasn't so bad. My big brother and sister came to see me, both teenagers by then. After you died, they became sort of surrogate parents. The man you married turned out to be an OK dad. As with a lot of men of that era, the domestic world was a foreign land to him. As you might expect, he was loving but remote, and with a hair-trigger temper. Does that sound familiar? Your oldest two children loved me. I feel certain that your love for them was so strong that it came through them to me.

In hospital, they brought food and treats and a book of stories about mythical and magical beasts. After they left, I did not feel like reading, but I looked at the pictures. Made up shows in my head about them. I felt like some kind of beast in a chrysalis. There was a barrel-vaulted wire frame over my legs to keep the covers up. I hid the book and the treats in there.

There were maybe thirty other kids in the ward, not counting those out on the balcony. When it was time for lights out, I knew the drill, as this was my second night. Sleep would be difficult, lying on my back. It was not quite dark enough to stare at nothing, but I tried. Over and over, the nurse kept pestering me to close my eyes.

As it was my second night on the ward, I knew I could endure all this. New situations were alarming to me, edged with the death of the known, but I was used to the ward now. Not so with the new kid. He was on the other side. I could not see much of him. He was younger than me, so already I regarded him with contempt. It seemed like he had gone to sleep. Then he woke up, frightened and alone. He called out for his mother. And would not stop.

The nurse on night duty did her best to calm him. Over and over, he kept calling and calling for her. A voice so desperate, so lost, a wail of absolute need. Nothing placated him. At first his cries had been animated, urgent. Then his cries settled into a rhythm of relentless, hopeless, animal pleading. As if he was pacing himself, as if he knew he would have to cry all night. And he did. He woke up most of the ward, calling and calling. Some of the other kids tried to calm him, but most yelled at him, told him to shut up. The nurse was trying to deal now both with this bereft child and with the rest of the ward, awake. I said nothing.

It took me fifty years, and transition, to figure this out: I was mad at that kid, and later I was ashamed of myself for not attending to his suffering. I was supposed to be on his side, but that night I wasn't. The feeling of shame about this took over the memory. I forgot why I was mad at him in the first place.

I expected to spend the night staring at the ceiling making up stories about Daleks, protected by the odd orange Dalek in revolt against all the others. The one who would not exterminate me for being awake. I was mad at him not for keeping me awake but because his mother would eventually come. You could not come for me. I was mad at him for having a mother to call out for when I did not.

Another thing I figured out after fifty years, in transition, is that what made it worse is not just that this boy alone in a hospital could call his mother and I could not call to you; it was also that it was in a hospital that I had last seen you. This is where you died. The hospital was like a bad Dalek, a gray and technical thing. And it had taken you. I was mad at this thing that had exterminated you.

This is why this night was worse than that one where my father told me you were dead. Here was this boy calling for a mother I could not call, in the place that had taken you. If I called out, I might be swallowed up in the void that took you too.

◆

The operation on the left leg did not go as well as the operation on the right. The pain did not stop. My surgeon, Gordon Kerridge, came in the middle of the night to the ward. For one thing, blood was seeping through the cast. A nurse drew with a marker around the spreading stain. It kept spreading, past the black line. The nurse put the "Nil by Mouth" sign back over my bed. The next day, hungry again, I went back to surgery, and they corrected whatever had not quite gone right.

After that, I stayed in hospital for some months. Both legs in casts. A time of boredom. They moved me onto the balcony where at least there was sunlight and the sound of the sea.

The other kids there were mostly in for the long haul too. I made friends with a boy my age. I visited on his bed; he visited on mine. We tried to hide out in the barrel-vaulted cage over my bed, but it was not quite big enough for the two of us and my casts. We sang each other our favorite songs. I forget mine. His was "Ring of Fire." He sang it quietly so the others didn't hear. He was in hospital for something to do with kidneys. He said that one day they would probably take him away in a black box, forever. One day he was gone and didn't come back. Nobody told me if the box they put him in was black, or not.

After some months, a man in a white coat disinterred my new feet from the casts with an electric saw. The skin inside was dry, reptilian. The feet did not look like my feet but some alien graft. Now began the long process of learning to walk. Like that first time, with you, with the casts. This time, without you, on crutches. The ground swam. I was a sea creature trying to evolve into a land creature all in one go. Day after day more exercises, to make me make the transition back into upright life.

It seemed to take forever, but then I was walking again. My walk was different. Odd at first, but as walking got easier, walking itself changed into something a bit more fluid. Running was still hard. "Wark can't run!" The other kids loved to laugh at that one. I could do a quick sprint, but that was it. Today, my feet still have no arches. My ankles barely rotate. I don't really have calves, as there's not much for the muscle to pull on. The operation was declared a successful experiment, nonetheless. I was a real biped now—or could pass for one.

Gordon Kerridge made my feet. They are little sculptures of meat that he and his team made for me. Their technique kept me upright for a long time. Fifty years later it is getting hard to walk again. I can't roam about and discover the byways of cities like I used to—but I still dance. Fifty years is a pretty good run for any tech.

◆

When I finally started transition, these unfamiliar stories, images, finally cut together. I had an edit of my memory now, as I edited my body. As much as anyone ever figures anything out, I figured out this: that I had buried Bow Girl, bound her deep, cut her from my script, refused the very notion of gender transition, because I had already been through one transition and could not bear the thought of another.

My transition happened when I was seven. A transition to being a biped. Or at least passing as one. I went into that antiseptic place that had killed you. I had the worst night of my little life. Not the night when I was told that you were dead. But the night when I was reminded that you would always be gone to me. I learned, in the place that took you, that it was pointless to even cry out.

I had been put in the care of experts who had done their best to change my body with experimental surgery. In my case, it worked, up to a point. But while knowing what something is like makes it less threatening and difficult for me, in the case of surgery, it's the opposite. I never wanted anything like it to ever happen again.

Or so I thought. But once I had this rough cut of my transsexual self, I felt the courage to contemplate at least some gender-transition surgeries. I decided to start with a simple outpatient procedure. With those, they send you home as soon as you can walk. No sleepless nights on the ward. My first surgical edit to my body would be an orchiectomy. It's a fancy way of naming a kind of castration. One where they just cut your balls off.

The preparation was all going swimmingly. The most emotionally difficult part had been wrangling the American health insurance racket. On the day before the operation, the instructions before the procedure don't say "Nil by Mouth" here, but it was the same thing. No food for twenty-four hours. I was hungry, but ready.

Christen took me to the hospital. It was back when we were still married, still living together. A different antiseptic smell that doesn't madeleine me back to the past. The colors and sounds are different too, all digital beeps and pips, bright and clear. The uniforms are different. They wheel me into the cold operating room. They put an electric blanket over me. Benign machines loom everywhere. Orange blinky lights. It's as bright as a television studio. All goes well until they lower a clear plastic mask over my face.

I've been told its just oxygen, that the anesthetic will be intravenous. The gas doesn't smell like anything. It's the mask that sends me back. This mask is clear plastic, but I remember, for the first time, that the mask that put me under when I was seven was black rubber. Smell of black rubber. I remember, too, that this was what made both the worst thing—and the second-worst thing—so much worse. The mask coming down.

The last few seconds of consciousness before blackout: fighting to stay awake. I close my eyes to concentrate. I can't resist. The last thing I remember is the feeling that this is what the final moment of consciousness might have been felt like for you. The black second where I am close to you again. At last. It's worse than all those other worst things—because part of me wants it.

Recovering from the orchiectomy was simple enough. A few days later I went out dancing. But no more surgeries for me—if

I can help it. I spent my life not quite passing as a biped, so I guess I have it in me to spend my later years not quite passing as a woman. Anyway, I am in my sixties now—a time of life you never lived to feel. As an old woman nobody really cares about my physical presence in the world, as any gender. I take hormones, dress femme, walk with a sway of the hip.

Occasionally I'm asked, in a threatening way: Are you a man or a woman? Since I can't really run away, I usually just answer: Yes.

Maybe I should just tell them my gender is orange Dalek. They might be made of cardboard and glue, and, like me, have an issue with stairs, but they are still the scariest thing in the world.

1.3

(To Sue)

It felt like a great honor to my seven-year-old self. I was to be one of the three kings in the school's Christmas fete. I already had a sword, which seemed like the sort of thing a king should have, for the beheadings and so forth. It was plastic and hollow, but this was all pretend so it would do.

There was a little dance we would do to the carol while the other kids sang it. "We three kings of Orient are." The words didn't make much sense, but the tune was pretty. I liked dress-up. I was learning to like attention. It filled a need.

The teacher in charge gave each of we three kings a square of black fabric. We were told to ask our mothers to sew it into a cape. Disaster. I didn't have a mother, so she could not sew my cape, so I could not be a king. Frozen into inaction. I didn't know what to say.

When I got home, I took to my bed and cried. Then you came to me, to ask what was wrong. You comforted me, told me everything would be alright. You could sew the cape for me. You were a mother to me. You were sixteen years old. You were and are my big sister. And something more than that.

There's a picture of the three kings, dancing in our capes, at the school fete. I suppose all the parents came, but I know nothing of that, or of who took the picture. Was it our father? I have no memory of him involved in any of these little rituals.

I tell people I was raised by teenagers. "Raised by wolves" as Christen, the mother of my kids, says. You did a great job of raising me, you and our older brother. I do a good impression of humankind.

There's a meme about how wolf packs travel. The strong, prime adults at the back, the kids in the middle, the old ones out front. So they don't get left behind, but also so they can scout ahead, use what they remember, what they lived through. That's me now.

◆

There's more of him in me than I like, but I just never related to our father. When we three siblings get together, we tell stories about him in a comic mode, but at the time his temper kept me permanently on edge. He gave me plenty of lessons in why it didn't pay to be too vulnerable. In his way he was generous, and I was spoiled rotten, but he never bought my love. By the age of twelve I was calling him by his given name—Ross—like a roommate.

When our mother died, I was about six, you fifteen, our brother seventeen. I thought you and our brother were grown-ups. Only later did I realize how young you were. Lugging a little kid around town as you tried to grow up yourselves. Since you were a girl, I thought of you in terms of mother. Since our father was still alive, I did not think of our brother in terms of father. There's asymmetry there, on top of the usual ones about these roles. I made cards for you on Mother's Day.

In summertime, you took me to Newcastle Beach. Long, sweltering bus rides from our Cardiff Heights home. The bus stop across the road, a square wooden pole painted mustard yellow. The green and yellow bus. On the bus: tiny rectangle tickets; that cindered smell. On the beach: The brightness of the light; the blueness of the sky. The sounds of waves and gulls, all summer. When I was little it seemed summer would last forever. That Christmas would never come again.

You in a bikini, working on your tan. Beach toys for me while I made up stories in my head. I was usually something else besides a human boy, some kind of animal. After the beach, a donut from Shipmates. I didn't like that it was near the hospital, but I loved to watch the donut machine. Bus back up Hunter Street, the main street back then, before the suburban malls drained it of life. Shopping at the cooperative, known as The Store. We had a charge account. You let me get magazines. Lunch at Illoura Hall, the cafeteria inside The Store, decorated with colored flouro tubes. My favorite was the meat pie with peas and gravy on top.

You were a model in a fashion show at The Store. You took me to the rehearsals in a warehouse nearby. Reading my books or coloring with my pencils, looking up whenever you came down the runway. You and some other models were supposed to toss a football to each other, but there wasn't one yet, so a box of tissues had to substitute.

The model of what a woman is supposed to be doesn't start with our mother. I barely remember her. It's you. When I'm shopping for clothes now, I'm always attracted to styles that hint at the mid to late sixties. Color blocks and geometrics; miniskirts and boots. The blue and green eyeshadow you favored. It could be read as all conventionally Freudian. The ambiguous, formless, ungovernable love of a child.

Once, when I was small, you tried to get me ready for a day and night with the little girl next door and her family. I liked them. The mom was patient, a schoolteacher. It was she who taught me how to tell the time. Their dad fixed a toy for me once, as unlike ours he had a workshop in the garage and proper tools. I liked the little girl too. We played with our dolls and stuffed animals, and made up all sorts of adventures for them.

This time I couldn't bear to be parted from you. I could sense your frustration. You were wearing nice clothes and makeup, maybe for a date. Now I'm thankful that you made time for yourself, that you didn't give in to my endless childhood neediness. Boundaries. Never any fun to learn.

You were magical to me. The one thing I wanted one birthday was Silly Putty. It was probably the thing advertised to kids on television at the time. It seemed unlikely I could have that, given our father's dislike for commercial television, for fads and various other things on which he had declarative opinions.

I was watching *Doctor Who* when you appeared before me, holding in one hand something concealed in purple velvet, and in the other, a silver magic wand. I knew the magic wand was your mascara, but in the moment, it was a magic wand. One thing can stand for another. You asked me to wish for what I wanted and wave the wand. And when I did, there was my desire.

I liked to be in your room when nobody was home. Everything in warm and dark colors. It was a bit chaotic, but you'd made that little space yours. First of a series of lush environments you will create—so different to the rest of our childhood home. Pictures cut from magazines on the walls. I remember one that said: "God is dead." Makeup supplies all over your dresser. The circular case for your contraceptive pills. I opened it and stared at them for a long time. Smooth little white pearls. I took one.

Was it you? Did I want to be you? Be like you? Or did I want to participate in the way of being in the world that you inhabited? Did I want to play with the technics of femininity? Was it some family psychodrama? Or is it just something buried in this flesh, that masculinity never feels right? Where does trans femininity come from? I don't know. I don't care. It doesn't matter.

I wanted to be you, but I also wanted to be Barbara Feldon, who played Agent 99 on *Get Smart*. I wanted to be you, but I also wanted to be Barbara Eden, who played Jeannie on *I Dream of Jeannie*. Above all I wanted to be Diana Rigg, who played Emma Peel on *The Avengers*. That was my favorite show. A surrealist spy caper, in which Emma would karate-kick the bad guys in her leather catsuit.

Femininity seemed something that could be anywhere, a pleasure of surfaces, a play of signs, one for another. The white dress Mick Jagger wore at the Brian Jones memorial concert.

Keith's shock of dark, full hair, rather like yours. Keith wore a lot of his girlfriend Anita Pallenberg's clothes. Mick came off all tough and macho in the songs, but who were these women, what was this femininity, that he was singing about? She might be under his thumb, but she got under his skin.

I got by in the slippage of how gender was supposed to appear, particularly as the sixties turned into the seventies and my teen years. Unisex styles were in, and I wore fitted stripey scoop-neck tops with ceramic pendants and wide-cut corduroy jeans in mauve or maroon or burgundy. Even after you left home, I carried on what I learned from shopping with you—and from looking through your wardrobe when you were out.

Our mother had a few volumes of the Hogarth Press *Standard Edition of the Works of Sigmund Freud*. I read them as a teenager. In the Freudian fairytale, it's fathers who are supposed to intervene between mother and child, breaking their symbiosis, standing in for the outside world. That's not what happened. Father was some random thing, temperamental weather. He worked and paid the bills. I once mentioned something, I forget what, that you'd bought at The Store when we went to do the shopping, and he flew into a rage about the expense. His role was to provide the means via which we absorbed and repurposed the limited repertoire of acceptable images and styles the spectacle offered for forging our own lives.

It's not your fault that I felt abandoned, and for the second time, when you left home to move to Sydney. I was a teenager by then. You expected our father to marry Melva, the widow with whom he'd formed a relationship, so that I wouldn't just be living with him. That never happened. Nor did they live together. She was an independent woman. Ran her own business. My unprovable theory about Melva and her first husband is that at least one of them was gay. She never had kids and didn't want to be anyone's stepmother. I got close to her for a little while, but she pulled away.

The last time us three siblings were together, we shared stories about our father, like the time he brought home the secretary he was fucking and you two told him—absolutely not. In the telling of those stories, you both referred to him as Dad and I referred to him as Ross. Which makes them different stories.

Maybe he didn't know much about being a father because he didn't have one. His father, our paternal grandfather, died when he was small. He was raised by what I think of as the "lesbian aunts." When I became a father, I had no idea how to be one either. How to wear that hollow crown. Raised by wolves. Raising wolf cubs in turn. I worry that I failed them. I hope at least that they will know, with mammalian certainty, that they were loved.

◆

I was in Princeton for a conference. Had gone to the dinner the first night. Woke up in the hotel next morning to a text message from Christen. She was in the emergency room with a burst ovary, but the situation was under control, she said, so I needn't come back. I ditched the conference and came straight to the hospital.

Hospitals terrify me, trip me into the worst dissociation. Christen in a narrow cot, partitioned off, pale, distressed, out of it on pain meds. The man in the next cot groaning and shouting "My johnson! My johnson!" A kidney stone, apparently. I thought of Montaigne, who had them. Birthing a kidney stone through your dick would give you a certain outlook on life.

Coming back from that moment of dissociation: I get mobilized for action. Get kids from school. Get them home and fed. Christen tends to micromanage when stressed, so I let her tell me what I was to make them for dinner, while quietly planning something else. So began our year together of Christen's cancer treatments.

Which she survived. But for a while there, that horrible feeling of scenes repeating in my life. One scene can become another. Now I'm the father who might lose a partner. Now it's my kids who might lose a mother. Now it's my oldest, just barely a teen, who has to step in to help out with the little one. And now my youngest might lose a mother before being old enough to form enduring memories of her. Like me. How fragile is this kind of privatized family. In denial of its dependence on whole worlds of hidden care.

Some years ago, my friend Shelly lay dying of cancer. She too had young kids. She asked me, based on my experience, what they would remember of her. This is the hardest question I ever had to answer. I said they would know that they were loved.

That was the year I was no longer a wolf. I had to become a human. Women in the neighborhood made meals for us. Some just left them on the doormat, so I wouldn't have to say anything. I accepted help. I cared for Christen. I cared for the kids. I sank into the labor of care. And somehow kept up the paid labor of teaching.

And I saw my oldest child step into the care for the younger one that you and our brother did for me. On top of this situation, which took reserves of strength I had not tapped for a long time, was the sudden inrush of the past. My past. This repetition. Like seeing the same scene played, over and over, but seeing it now from another character's point of view. I never wanted to be like our father. But now I was cast in his role, in the same plot. The same misery.

The story turned out differently. In this version, the mother recovers. Christen's first thought was to get out of our marriage. My first thought was to get out of masculinity. Both those things took a while. What we actually did right away was get cats.

"Ask Daddy if she fed the cats," says Christen to one of the kids. I'm still a dad, with she/her pronouns. Christen will aways be the mother. The one who gestated, birthed, and nursed them. I respect that. "Mother" is different to "mothering." Anyone can do the mothering. Maybe everyone could have some share in it, in that mode of care. Although it turns out I'm destined to be Dad in the sense of the one who pays the bills.

Mothering can also be a job. When my mother got sick, Mrs. Fisher started coming to help. Made my soft-boiled egg with toast soldiers in the morning. I called her Fishy. Some days I was at her home. Her husband had a stable. Everything smelled of horses. The house was full of ribbons from horse shows. The Fishers were from another time, before the suburb was built around them. Before the postwar boom. Those remaindered by a new economy are the hired help to fill in the familiar dysfunctions of the new one.

◆

I learned something about writing. That one thing can become another. A square of black fabric becomes a cape. A box becomes a football. A sister can mother. A father can mother. A boy can be a wolf if you let him. A boy might even become a woman. She might prefer becoming a woman to being a king.

This power, for one thing to become another—to me it's a certain power of femininity. Its power is not strong. Its power is to use all available avenues to avoid capture as long as it can, to avoid being under his thumb. I didn't much want to be king. I just wanted to write my own fairy tales.

It seemed unlikely I'd be a writer. In second grade I got detention for my poor handwriting. The class was ranked by reading ability, and I got a C, which meant I could not read the books on the A or B shelves. I took the book about wolves from the A shelf while nobody was looking.

Because I was raised by wolves, there was a certain amount of cunning involved. The time Ross forbade us to go to the beach, but we went anyway. You hustled me into the shower to wash off the sand just as he was pulling up. Or the time I broke the glass on the Ruth Tuck watercolor. You swept up the glass and we pretended nothing had happened. Ross never noticed.

You and I driving home from the beach. In my memory it's in a convertible. Did any of your boyfriends own a convertible? You wear aviator shades and a shirt (his?) over your bikini to ward off the sun. There's a strike at the refinery, so gas, or petrol as we'd call it, is in short supply. You pull into a service station to talk the attendant into letting you get some. You took the shirt off first. He obliges. As we drive away, I ask why you did that. You just give me a look.

You were photographed by some beach photographer and became a "page three girl" in the local tabloid, in your bikini. The story gave your name. There weren't many Warks in the phone book. Men started calling, driving Ross to distraction. I answered one of those calls, when nobody was around. He asked if I'd seen you naked, and I had, in the bath. Many years later I realized I'd been listening to a man jerk off over the phone to a description of you by a child.

Femininity has a power—a slight one—but it is punished for this power. And not just by men. I was learning this already. If I was called a girl at school, it was as prelude to being pushed to the ground. By boys, but some of the girls would join in the laughter. Some of those girls grew up to think they are feminists.

After you left Newcastle, I'd take the train to Sydney to come visit you some weekends. Your flat with your boyfriend, right on Bondi Beach, back when such a thing was still possible. My little provincial self, learning the ways of twentysomething sophisticates in the Big City. And learning from you how to smoke pot.

Learning too about my own femininity. Several times, men approached me, on the train, in the station. Their desire laced with pleasure and danger. It was a while before I'd know how to extract what I might want from such situations without consequences. I wanted them to want me, but also to avoid ending up subject to their moods.

The one thing I wanted from them was to feel, in their attention, like a girl. I didn't want them at all. I wanted men to look at me the way they looked at you. And they did, or almost. Not the same look. More furtive, lupine. A look I'll come to know well. I might be a wolf, but I'm nobody's bitch.

Lovers

2.1

(To Mu)

I don't remember how I found you, Mu; I remember how I lost you. Sydney, the eighties, our twenties, we jostle in the stream of the city. Chance encounters at parties, in bars, at shows, in clubs. The inner city was still our playground. It was cheap, not yet retrofitted for the high-price urban economy to come.

When I met you, I was still in school, getting my MA at the University of Technology, Sydney, in that brutalist tower right by Central railway station. The communications school there was where all the new stuff was happening. Piecing together a living writing for magazines, making radio, adjunct teaching. Doing my coursework while working the graveyard shift at Numbers, the glory hole place on Oxford Street.

Around the time we met, I got my first full-time job at *On the Street*. Four of us did a forty-eight-page rock and roll magazine and gig guide every week. Paid in cash under a false name. I wrote, edited, copy-edited, photo-edited, wrote captions, did some layout, answered phones and, above all, took in the listings from the pub managers. *On the Street* was known on the street as *In the Gutter*—which is indeed where you could find our tiny staff some mornings.

It was a terrible job, but it had its benefits. The paper went not just to the venues but the rehearsal studios. Musicians read it. Since my byline was in it, I had entrée to the clubs. It was focused on live music, but the nightclubs advertised in it too, and wanted coverage. The clubs were where we went when the pubs shut. And when those shut, we went to the all-night Taxi Club, where the dawn of day met the twilight of desire.

I didn't meet you at the Taxi. You had more sense than to end up there. I remember you at Commotion, and maybe Berlin or Stranded, and The Freezer, that one just east of Taylor Square on Oxford Street where Andy Glitre often DJed. A straight club, which I'd go to before walking west to the gay part of Oxford Street, to work my shift at Numbers.

Taxi Club is where I met Clementine and took her home. Her place was way out west. Mine, much closer, was in Ultimo, on the western lip of the city center. I was embarrassed about going to mine as it was such a mess, but she didn't care. And I was embarrassed for less defensible reasons: Clementine was trans.

Back at mine, we made out, inconclusively, both very drunk. And there she was, sleeping it off in my bed. I was restless. Usually, the pain of desire was that the women I wanted I also wanted to be. An impossible desire. The desire to be you, for instance. Now, I wanted Clementine and wanted to be her—and I could. A blind curve opens in the maze. I couldn't sleep. I let her sleep for a while. Told her I had to go to work, which was a lie. Coffee, no breakfast. I forgot all about it. Or so it seemed.

Transsexuality is the shock of the possible.

I didn't see you at the Taxi, but I saw you around. Your friends knew my friends. I vaguely remember you hitting on me rather than the other way around. Our first date was in my flat. I had, still have, rudimentary skills at it, but I like to entertain. You brought flowers. I made dinner. We kissed. You went home. Somehow, we ended up together. I became a fixture in your big share house in Newtown. Mingling with your flatmates. I'm still Facebook friends with the painter.

Your parents ran a grocery store; my father was an architect. Like me, you were supposed to get a law degree. The height of petit bourgeois parental ambition was that the kids become doctors or lawyers. We were law school dropouts. Our ambitions weren't about lapping the partner track. We wanted revolution.

The means at our disposal were cultural. One theory popular at the time was that the cultural superstructures had some autonomy from the capitalist economic base. As cultural workers in the superstructures, we could combine theory and practice to make a different kind of media, as the means to undo the dominant ideologies from within.

The technical tools at our disposal were analog, and cheap. Everyone had a guitar or drum machine or video camera. Enter the kitchen of a share house and there'd be those beautiful political screen-print posters from Redback Graphics. The community radio station, 2SER, played while we prepped and ate communal meals. Then maybe we'd go to Performance Space or Art Space or Art Unit, or to see the Super 8 movies at the Filmmaker's Coop. Or see a friend's band at the pub, and then to the clubs.

The internet wasn't a big thing yet, but there were already global flows of interesting art and media, to be found in Gleebooks or Phantom Records or that cool video store. The metropolitan centers of London, New York, Paris and Tokyo left their calling cards in each. The previous generation were the last whose escape from the provinces, real or imagined, looked to London. We were more interested in Paris for theory, New York for art, Tokyo for its astonishing synthesis of city and image worlds.

You worked for an organization that made educational materials, mostly in audio format, on multiculturalism—still official state policy. And low-key feminist material for girls. I was still at *On the Street*, just about to become part of a collective that would restart the radical journal *Intervention*. You joined another collective, making another journal called *Third Degree*. Everybody we knew was making something.

For straight people of means, this life was vaguely understood to be temporary. We were supposed to get real jobs, put a down payment on some place a bit further out in the inner western suburbs. Have some kids. That didn't happen to you and me. Different twists. In my case, even though I had very little conscious notion about it, the twist could be named Clementine.

It's probably not uncommon, in one's twenties, to fail to have relationships that last. For me it usually didn't work out past the two-year mark. Twice around the sun. When you're with someone you want to fuck and love, but whom you also want to be—it's complicated. Messy breakups. Boyfriends in between. And chemsex with Edward, my first real boyfriend—who I'd return to so he could fuck me. That went on with Edward for thirteen years. As if that could keep the possible girl in me possible—a latent other self.

With you, Mu, it was physical. We fucked a lot. I was terrible at it. I was lucky to have had sexually confident girlfriends, of which you were maybe the third. Actually, it wasn't luck. I was bad at seduction. Bad at expressing interest, uncomprehending of anyone's interest in me. I could respond only to women who were sexually direct. None of this is a mystery anymore. Women who wanted me responded to a masculinity I had but didn't want or to a femininity I also had but could barely express.

Being terrible at straight fucking and being with sexually confident women, I had to learn. I was willing to learn. They taught me. You taught me. If I couldn't be a woman, I could at least get lost in the details of your body, be attentive to its wants and needs. I needed moves. I'd get hard fast, and in those days reliably, but I'd cum in just a few minutes. I had to learn what to do with mouth and fingers.

Why is it that I remember sex more clearly than nearly anything else? But then also such strange memories. The memory of being present but lost in that presence, hence no memory of anything specific. And: the memory of not being present—now I'd say dissociating—so remembering the specifics clearly but nothing about how I felt about it. Cutting a story together from empty frames.

We'd make out in your room or mine. You'd leave for a minute, to insert your diaphragm. You never wanted me to see that. We'd fuck—briefly. As prelude. The thing you liked most, given my limitations, was to straddle me, cowgirl style, and rub your clit along my limp dick. In those days, before hormones subtly changed all my senses, the sight of you doing this was everything. That and the feel of your skin as I held your hips. That and the feeling of your sexual use of me got me going, and we'd fuck again.

◆

"Give me your money!" It's a thing you said to everyone you cared about. You said it to me many times. Some people thought it was a bit, a joke, a quirk. To me it felt like something else. Both ironic and sincere at once, as was your style. What's love in an age that appears as a vast accumulation of commodities? It's the money, but also the negation of money—revolution. What you said: "Give me all your money!" What I heard: "I need love and revolution!"

Yours was a wry love for the world around. At a party at Gregory's place, everyone dancing. When Do-Ré-Mi's song "Man Overboard" came on, many of the women present sang it to each other. It's a brilliant song about a boring, self-involved boyfriend, who could have been about many of us there. You stood watching, and remarked: "They think it's feminism, but they're just mad that they're straight."

The most important thing in your life, besides revolution, was other women, particularly your two closest friends, Clare and Tania. The three of you had committed yourselves to a project of complete emotional honesty and mutual support. I was jealous. Which was probably why I showed up uninvited at Clare's house, with unclear motives. You forgave me; she didn't.

The love you shared with Clare and Tania mattered to you as love was the hard thing to find and keep in your life. Your mother was alive, but unstable. And unhappy. She led a very isolated life. She'd come straight from the village, and the Cantonese she spoke was a dialect that set her apart, even in Sydney's expansive Cantonese-speaking world. I only met her once. She chatted away to you in her dialect, and you answered, mostly in English, while she threw a fish and some ginger in a wok and did it to perfection.

Lying in bed one night, after we'd fucked, you said, into an easy silence: "I love you." After a pause, I said, "I don't know what to do with that." Which was true. Even though I already loved you back. It frightened me. I'd never fallen in love before. All I knew about love was abandonment. These sound like excuses. What I know is that I was afraid. You had the courage to love, and I didn't. I failed to meet you in that place of vulnerability you offered me. And for that, you never forgave me.

◆

I failed you. So did the world. You felt the mood of the wider culture change. You felt not just its ordinary, everyday racism, but the rise of a kind of surplus racism. Not that it was ever easy being Chinese in Australia, but toward the end of the eighties, it got worse.

The official policies of multiculturalism still centered whiteness. Sure, everyone could have their specific culture, but it was white people like me who were empowered to speak for the culture as a whole. It was just another language for white supremacy. You knew this. Would remark on it with your wry humor. Worked within it to work against it. But it got to you when the level of racism jumped. The bus driver who told you to go back to where you came from. You deadpanned: "One ticket to Newtown, then." The man who spat at you while shopping. The beer can thrown from a passing car as we held hands on King Street. You no longer imagined you could ever belong.

I got sick, terribly sick for a while. The official diagnosis was "Ross River fever," as nobody could figure out what else it could be. This disease of the rural economy hypothetically transmitted to me by mosquito because Ultimo, where I lived, was near Paddy's Market, where livestock was still sold. I'll never forget how you nursed me through those horrible cold-sweat nights. I think that's when you got me the pink bear that was the twin of Milk Carton, the blue stuffed animal that you held each night in your bed.

Eventually my family came and got me. When you came up to Newcastle unannounced to see me, they gave you the coldest reception. My father more because he could never handle spontaneity, lived by schedules and routines. But then there was Melva's undisguised racism. You didn't stay. I'd have left with you if I could have moved. A petty allegory for how you can't leave whiteness.

You went to China, enrolled in a course in Chinese medicine in Beijing. But that didn't feel like home either. In your letters you wrote about dropping out. Falling in with expats—in those days kept at arm's length, in a special enclave. Living with Rachel, another ex of mine who was there as the partner of a newspaper correspondent. Working as a PA on the movie *The Last Emperor*. Getting arrested. Didn't have your passport. Beijing cops took you for an undocumented migrant from the south. You felt no more at home in Beijing than Sydney.

I heard you set off traveling, on the Trans-Mongolian Express, to Berlin. I got to Beijing just as you left. I'd wanted to see you. Wanted you back. To make amends. I couldn't get the visas to follow, so I stayed in Beijing. I lived rent free, as you had been, in the enormous apartment my ex's journalist boyfriend had as part of his job, which he liked to keep filled with interesting people to amuse him.

I lived off savings and the occasional bit of writing. Fascinating city, shaped by decades outside of capitalism, just about to change. Wary of the self-described dissidents, assumed to be informants, I wandered the streets by day, feeling their ambience, open to chance encounters. After dark, even here, finding night people. I played the role of a curiosity in exchange for gracing tables.

After about six months of this life, I heard a rumor that I'd been offered a full-time teaching job at University of Technology, Sydney. I'd applied before I left, just for the practice. Some misadventure had befallen the favored candidate, and so they were looking for me. Me, who had never had a legal full-time job, and had barely finished a master's degree. That was what brought me back to Sydney and accidentally started my academic career, such as it is.

On your return from your travels, back in Sydney, you moved into the Love Hotel—a huge, open warehouse on Parramatta Road in which everyone lived on little covered platforms, reached by ladders, up in its eaves. A legendary place, more or less a commune, subsidized by raves on the vast open floor.

I wanted to get back together, but you were done with me. I'd not had the courage to love you the first time and did not deserve a second chance. I even brought you money once, up in your eyrie. In one of those red and gold gift envelopes you could get in Chinatown. Soon enough, you were traveling again.

◆

I was in my office at uni, poring over a pile of newspapers, full of news from Beijing. Gorbachev had come to meet with Deng, summit of the two great Communist powers, summoning an international media entourage. The students and others seized that visibility to occupy Tiananmen Square, setting off a weird global media event. Our mutual friend Shelly, Gregory's girl-friend, came to tell me of your death. A shock reaction to the malaria medication you took in Guatemala. Shelly and I held each other and wept. You were twenty-five years old.

Your family sat on one side of the church, and your friends on the other. We'd all passed by the open coffin. You held Milk Carton in your dead hands. The Baptist preacher spoke of the passage to heaven as a plane flight to a distant land. Given that you had died so far from home, this was too much.

Your friend Clare sang "Song to the Siren," a song your friends all knew. The urge was there in me to flee this scene, to dissociate. Her voice, that song, this gathering, the feeling of being bound to life, and having no escape from it.

After the service, Tania weeping. I reach out to hold her. She stiffens. Then looks at me and comes into my arms. Grief erasing some of the past tension between us. What overrides it is a pain we shared. Your close friends, too, were all feeling a little of what I felt: that we had all failed you. That none of us were up to your cool and total challenge to love. "You were her first love," Tania says to me. And you were mine. On our first attempts to reach out to another human, it was me who had failed, completely.

At the wake, at the Love Hotel, we shared stories. What I remember is how tenderly we tried to hold your extremes. Your compassion and harshness. Your confusion and clarity. Your joy and your tears. Your silence and outspokenness. Your sly humor and wry critique. And then also your leaps into loves that met no bounding opposite.

Clare and Tania presided over your effects. They gave me your last diary. There's a dream about me in it, although it is from a long time after we broke up. In it, my cock grows into a huge cone. Also among your effects: a check from the English boyfriend you'd had in China, uncashed. Also: a telegram I'd sent you one day, when I heard you were sad and feeling small: "reasons to be cheerful stop you are still taller than Deng Xiaoping stop." At five foot one, only by an inch. And the rubber stamp I'd had made for you that said "MU TEAM." You were Mu and we were all your team. We all felt the wound in you. We all tried to heal it. I failed. I know others feel that they did too.

One or two at a time, we'd mount the ladder to your bed. Smell the scent you'd left on your clothes. Your friends left me and Rachel alone up there to give us time to grieve that part of our grief that connected us three. Rachel talked about traveling in China with you. You'd been close, I knew. I didn't know in what ways. She spoke of adventures, and then suddenly of the beauty of your shoulders. We kissed, hard, fast, tore clothes off, threw our bodies at each other. It wasn't sex, just a lust for life in memory of your living being. Trying to salve the bruise in our flesh of your absence. Then we lay together, held each other, and cried for a good long while.

◆

I still have your diary. And I keep a framed picture of you where you can look at me as I work. To keep me to the task in which we once both believed. To make writing, to make art, to make media, for the revolution, in whatever unknown form it might take. I still love this other thing that you loved. That you loved the world, and everything in it, and all it can be. Maybe I lost the faith that we could win. But I'll never lose my love of the world. I'll never not love what you loved. I won't fail. I can't fail. Even if I failed in my love for you. Even if we fail to heal the world.

And if ever I have loved, and allowed myself to be loved, you are there a little. One just has to love without expectations. Just give in without hope, and then love will be without fear. Love's no bargain. There's no exchange, no transaction, with the world. One just tries and fails to give, no receipts. One just trusts in a capacity to exceed oneself and open oneself; to go, to let go. In love, there's no happy endings. Only the memory of moments when what can be—was. Besides the memory of loss, there's those other memories, sometimes hard to feel, of all that giving. To accept what's given to us can be the hardest thing in the world.

"Love is not enough," you said, even though for you sometimes it was also too much. It's not enough to save the world.

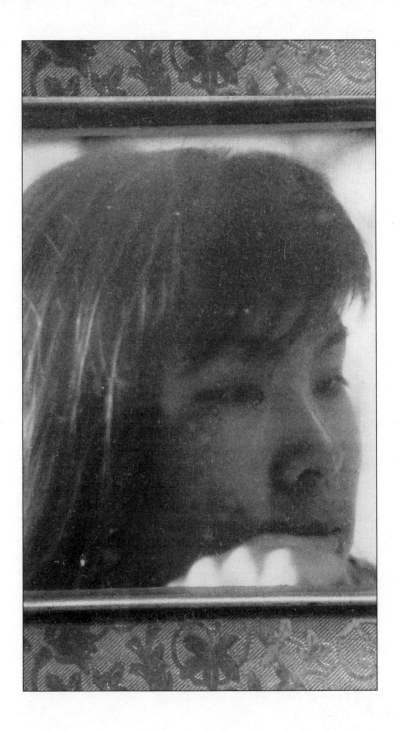

(To Christen)

I'd never seen your studio, Christen, your "room of one's own." Out in Newark, across the river. You'd go out for the day and spend the night there, to be away from the kids, but mostly away from me.

When I saw it, I felt the why of it. The light pouring in through the big windows. Shelves of your most-loved books. Little collections of pretty rocks and feathers. A station for art supplies, another for the sewing machine. Images from your great *Interiors* series on the wall. Risograph print of you naked and pregnant with our firstborn, the red and the blue not quite registering. You made a space that's yours alone, outside the wombat burrow of our shared life in Queens.

The light lunch you brought to share, nuts, dried fruit, lettuce, and quinoa. Then you show me around. It's an old office building that's now artist studios. You show me the empty one you want to use today for the photos. Dusty, but it too has good light. We drag the sofa from your studio to it.

It's our twentieth wedding anniversary. The traditional gift is china. Presumably because the happy couple will have smashed the last of the wedding gift set by then.

◆

It was your idea that our gift to each other would be to come out to your studio and spend the day together. I've done my face, and you've improved it. My skills are low-femme basic. I wish I'd done my nails. I brought several dresses, some formerly yours. I put the pink Ulla Johnson one on first.

Some house music, a Honey Dijon mix. These beats are opti-
mistic, convivial, gay. Techno makes you anxious. The slower
boom-chick of house is an ambience we can share. You arrange
both me and the ring light. You're directing. I move where you
want me. Honey smooths out the staccato time of posing.

"Work your angles," you tell me, and I adjust the 3D planes
of my bony face to the 2D plane of the camera. Modeling is
cubism in reverse. "Show me Sally and Susie." Huh? Oh, my
tits. I wonder if you're replaying lines photographers said to
you back when you modeled. In play are my need to be seen
as a woman and your need to be a woman who makes others
see what she sees.

There's so many ways, over these twenty years of a marriage,
that the asymmetry on which it was structured—failed. You
resent me for all of them, whether I'm at fault or not. Since I
transitioned, I can't bear the blade of your resentment, your
rage against life.

The kids have complicated teenage needs for us now, not
daily care. You survived cancer. I transitioned. The question
becomes, my dear: Who are we to each other now?

The pink dress looks particularly lovely on the blue sofa. It's
dusty, but that won't show. You want my crip feet in the frame,
so you have to clean the soles with a paper towel. It is entirely
possible that I fell in love with you when you said that you
liked my feet. Nobody else ever said that. Shuddering, they're
so sensitive. Along the scars is the worst, but even the soles.
Being touched there is more sensory overload than being ass-
fucked with my favorite dildo. Not that you've fucked me in
a while.

You want to include some paintings you made in the images.
They're hand-painted signs like the ones you make for protests.
They're all the things you felt about my transition that you
didn't want to say. Things you spent days and nights out here,
alone, painting on these bits of cardboard. The one I'm holding
is in black-edged white lettering on eggshell blue:

I look at her. I don't yell: "Your smell is gone! Your orchiectomy is a choice! Don't leave me! I love you! I have always"—I eat the cookies.

That one makes me cry. This one, in mauve, pink, cyan and rust, makes me laugh:

She says I blame her for everything. Doesn't everyone? I don't want to be an asshole, but I am expected to supply unwavering support when the goalposts are constantly changing. PLUS: She fits into my Betsey Johnson slip-dress from the 90s. Unforgiveable.

I pulsed through a dozen or so feelings about the signs. One is that you trust me to see them, which makes me imagine that even as we drift apart, some layer of shared life between us is still possible.

I don't think my transsexuality was any surprise to you. Not exactly straight, but not exactly gay, a life awaiting the negation of the negation that is transition. You knew as much as I did about it. I think. Is that conviction true? Anyway, it's not, or not the only, reason you want to separate.

You have a dress you want me to wear. Rose print, in silk. High neck, short sleeves. Not my style at all. I slip it on anyway. Fits well enough. It was your mother's. She made it herself. You take pictures of me in it.

Some emotional circuit closes, although I don't think either of us really knows what feelings are current. We both lost our mothers young. The hole that left in both of us drew us together, but neither could fill that absence for the other.

Our kids nearly lost you. I can't bear to think about that, so in my mind your cancer is gone and will never come back. I keep it together through my faith that you will outlive me. I'm ten years older, so the odds would have been in favor, but we are just playthings of unknown gods.

There's a familiarity with love and death that's a level where we connect.

"If you die first," I say, "I'll write you a really good eulogy. Funny and loving and short."

"If you die first, I'll write you a good one too—"

"Listing all of my faults, and *very* long."

You remember all those things, and I don't. I can't stand to see myself as you see me when you resent me. Some of the things you hate me for are real. I said and did those things. I get to think well of others, and of myself, and even you, by forgetting evidence to the contrary.

Actually, I do remember some things you said. "I love you, but I wish I didn't." Or that time you said, "Why didn't you transition years ago when I still wanted to talk to you?" That one I feel has comic genius.

We met in Williamsburg in the nineties. I was subletting from your Australian roommate. Then: we were long distance, for a few years. You'd come to Sydney; I'd come to New York. And then: we met up in London, to see if we had a future. Romance along the routes of empire.

Married in Sydney. We exchanged the silver rings we had wrought. Mine convex, yours concave. They fit together. We switched the vows. The celebrant asked you: "Do you take this woman …?" And asked me, "Do you take this man …?" And yet how easily we fell into an order of things that we didn't think we wanted, as man and wife, where I played the man, or at least butch to your femme.

Harron says there's three genders: straight, dyke and faggot. Having tried all three, maybe I'm somewhere in between all of them, leaning a bit dyke-ward. And you?

I emigrated. Had to start over, in American academia, at nearly forty. Touch and go until I landed a full-time, three-year (renewable) contract to teach undergrads at the New School, a job that became my life.

Two kids, but I don't like to write about them. Now that

they are teenagers, parenting becomes dialectical. They need us as something that they can negate, overcome and supersede.

And now, in your studio, who are we? I was a man, I was a husband, I was a father. Now I'm the woman our kids call Dad. But who am I to you? Who are we to each other? Co-parents, of course. And? I don't know the genre of what's to come. We pack up the dresses and you drive us back to what is still home. This was before you ask me to leave it.

◆

A week or so later, we go to the lake house. We rent it every year for summer commune with parent friends. We take your car. After years of resisting, I relented, gave you the money to buy a Subaru, the iconic lesbian ride. From a sort-of-straight hook-up to a sort-of-lesbian breakup—that was our road movie.

The lake house is where, just a few summers prior, I went up to the top of the hill, took mushrooms and made the decision to transition. Late transition is a funny thing. Diana thinks there are only two kinds of trans people: those who can hide it and those who can't. Those who can't have to shiv out of the shell of an assigned sex before they have the resources or the wiles to work out how to survive in the cis world. Those who can hide it do their—our—best at appearing in the cis world. We might even fancy we belong there. Maybe some of us do. With luck we figure out how to come out without exposing ourselves to destruction. I'm one of the ones who hid, even from myself, for the longest time.

At the lake house. This time, we leave the kids with others and take mushrooms together, down by the water's edge. You take the inflatable unicorn out on the water, your element, to drift in the sun, to watch the trees sparkle. I plunge into the deep, the cold depths of sadness. Feel the pull of the Kelvin-cold far below.

By temperament, I'm warm but distant: a comedic worldview, and under that, run cold. I first touched coldness when my mother died. Today, not buoyant, struggling up from coldness, back up from the deep, through other layers, cold but not so icy. The merely cool sadness of ordinary failure, of trifling time, life let by. That I left it so late to become a woman that this life as a woman will be very brief.

You are out of the water, dragging the unicorn behind you by its inflatable horn. You find me crying on the shore. You hold me. I can't really talk about it, the depths, the cold. I get a few words out, but the torrent is so swift it drags language under. You tell me—and you are far wiser in these things—that feelings aren't facts. You tell me that, all the same, emotions tell us something. Just listen and learn. You tell me this sadness will pass again, for a while.

"Did you always know that I was this sad person?"

"Of course. Just as I knew you were some other sort of gender."

"I don't think those things are connected, though."

"I'm just saying that I knew one just as I knew the other."

◆

If I live to be eighty, I'll inject estrogen—estradiol valerate—into my ass one thousand more times—a total of two liters of that oily suspension.

Sure, I've burned through more years than are to come, but living them now has this dense intensity, as more and more past resonates in present lived time.

I need you to outlive me. Unlike my mother, I need you to remain as you were from the start: robust, vital. I need you to be more resistant to the chill than me, than my body. But like my mother, you got cancer, and about the age she did. And all through the trials of your treatment I had to believe you would live to bury me. I didn't get to go to my mother's funeral, and I am not going to yours.

◆

Every marriage is a misrecognition. Things really get interesting when you recognize that. Not that you arrive at the truth of each other. It's more a matter of casting aside the first misrecognition and finding ones that can replace it. Maybe the misrecognition on my part was that you could be a woman in the world in my place. That I wouldn't have to do it myself. You were taller than me, stronger than me, prettier than me, and decidedly more fish.

And yet my love for you ran deep, plunged right into the coldness. Nothing about the ways in which it mistook you makes it any less true. That's the hardest part. That love can be so absolutely real and yet not recognize itself or that which it loves. It's the realest thing, and yet it connects lovers who never know either themselves or each other. When love is in crisis, it exposes our unreality to ourselves. I is a-nothing.

◆

We pack up and drive home from the lake house to New York City. The next day, we take the Subaru to downtown Manhattan for Reclaim Pride. It's just the two of us as the kids don't want to come. You drop me to park the car. This is where a handful of us gathered, only a summer before, to say the name of Layleen Xtravaganza Cubilette-Polanco—who died in solitary, imprisoned at Rikers, while the guards joked and laughed and ignored her cries.

Pride flags all ashimmer. I text you to find me under a solitary red flag of some Trotskyist sect. They offer me their literature, which I decline. They will be right about everything. They always are.

It's hard to recognize people with masks on. We talk to Tom for a bit. I get a text from Jessie, go off to find her. Jessie gives me her spare safety razor. I'm touched she remembered to bring it for me.

The march is about to begin. I find you, but you've lost Tom and I don't know where the others are now. I just want to be here with you. We're near the drummers, so we can dance down the streets, past City Hall, up along a winding route to Washington Square. The two of us in a crowd of maybe fifty thousand. We see Nash and I give her a hug. With masks on, so I guess that's fine.

The trans people I relate to are mostly younger than me. There's so few from my era. A lot are dead, or went deep stealth, or have what the younger ones think are outdated notions. I surround myself with mostly thirtyish, mostly artsy—but also mostly middle-class, mostly white—trans people. (The divisions of race and class don't spare our little worlds.) Who are they to me? An inspiration. Who am I to them? I don't know.

Feet starting to give out. You tell me the car is near, so we peel off. We decide to take the car to the gay end of Riis Beach. This is the summer I feel I can return to beach culture, after a forty-year absence, so long as we go to the beach that's what Alex calls faggot-space.

And it is. The pride flags fly from beach forts. Watching all this beauty. What I see as a tall, Black trans woman wanders up the beach and back down again. In a black one-piece, junk untucked.

"That used to be me," you say. "Walking on the beach to get attention. To get people to look at me."

"I'll bet it worked."

What I read as some Black cis gay men laugh together, touch each other. Two of them peel off to play catch, and one occasionally lands on top of us. He is so beautiful I don't even mind. "It seems I'm still attracted to men," I tell you quietly, "but only if they are really, really hot."

Yes, I know. It's problematic: the way this man's Blackness is implicated in how I see the beauty of his body. His tight ass rounding in his Speedos. His orange du-rag flapping in the breeze like an untied tongue. Can't catch or throw though. That perfectly toned body a gym artifact. A work of aesthetics rather than athletics.

I want to be physically close to you. Up till now, that closeness could still range into the sexual. But I don't feel you feel me that way anymore. I don't want to even try, as I don't want to compromise this marsupial closeness while we still have it.

I don't know my body anymore. I was just figuring it out, fucking other people, mostly other trans women, before the COVID-19 lockdown ended all that. We've had an "open marriage" for a long time. You'd used that dispensation in the past and I hadn't. I took it up only after I came out.

It's on the beach that I feel for the first time that the relation between our bodies is changed now and forever. It's for the best. Things have been good between us lately, but I'm always waiting for you to swing back to resenting me, and since transition, I don't feel emotionally strong enough to withstand that. I no longer have that steely breastplate of masculinity over my heart to protect me from my feelings about your feelings.

Storm clouds form and pass us by. It's cooler now. Such a day. A movie we starred in. Time to drive home.

The next day, you want to go to your studio to have some time away from me and the kids. I feed them and clean up after them. COVID lockdown life. The four of us in this little one-bathroom apartment. Now the kids and I all have our headphones on. I find home in an Elysia Crampton track Jessie shared with me, one that cuts through to me too, through warm and cold layers. The clang of armor falling from my body.

This body I sometimes call mine is sometimes off, somewhere else. Inside the sound now, the sound of geological layers and eons. Geological strata of sound and flesh. How temporary. That I feel so temporary in this world doesn't matter when I feel how temporary it too will be.

I found a way to be, and even if I found it too late, I have few regrets. I got to live a big part of my whole life with you. What times we had! What times we forget. What times we still have in us, in each other, otherwise, our unforgiven life.

I want you to see and sense who I'm becoming, but I'm afraid you won't like me anymore. Or love me. I want you to touch the worlds I wander into—selectively. It was awkward the first time you met my girlfriend, Jenny. The one after the random hook-ups, after the rebound affair where I felt loved but could not love. After the hook-ups again after that. Jenny is the one with whom I dance. The one who loves and whom I can now love. This new misrecognition, tender and fresh.

◆

For the longest time, before I transitioned, before I felt like I'd found passages through the labyrinths of love and money, sex and death, I felt like I had to keep track of any little thing that might hurt us, might set us back. Armored against outrageous fortune—and braced also for your occasional attacks from inside the fortress of middle-class anxieties. Now all I care about is that you, me, the kids, get to swim in the current, feel intensely, love freely, elaborate the arts of life—here, in the beautiful struggle.

What changed my disposition? So many things: these hormones, this love, the epidemic, our money, your survival. That there's only now and not much future.

But I have a question: "How do you see us, in the future?"

"We're having thanksgiving together, somewhere in the country. The kids are there, and maybe they bring loved ones. There's you and your partner, and me and mine, and we come together and share thanksgiving, even though we all live our own lives."

Here is where, for me, the political is personal. What fight is left in me is for a world where we will all sit together at thanksgiving—all those we love, and a spare seat as well for whoever needs it.

(To Jenny)

We go to sleep early, to get up early, to go to the rave. It's 4:00 a.m. We eat light, get caffeine into our bodies. Drop edibles. Pick outfits. We wear light jackets. It's spring, but not warm yet. We pack rave bags. Check for the location. Call a car. Dark streets, indigo night, shiny stars.

Doorman knows us. Love his energy. Quick hug and we're in. Our glasses fog. We can't see anything. We hear everything. Feel everything. We bring a bin liner for jackets. We bag the jackets and hide them. We greet friends and hug them. We buy water. We put in earplugs. We're ready.

We always go to the front. We like the feel of the sub bass. We like the breeze off the big bin. We try to find that place. That place in movement. It takes a while. We move into the sound. We let sound into flesh. We're moving but we're not there yet.

We hate everyone around us. All other humans are annoying as fuck. They have their phones out. They talk loudly. They won't let the beat in, won't let it fuck them. They are joined at the hip, the couple form, ignoring all others, zagging across the room like a Roomba.

We try a different spot. It's better here. Less annoying. Now it feels good. Everyone here is dancing. We are all dancing. Dancing is all we are. We sense each other's bodies and let a little of each other in. We are in this together. Whatever this is. It's time where everything is a friend.

How long have we been here? How long are we dancing? How did we get here? Into this other wave. We are in a pocket in time where there's more time. We are in a sideways time, spooling off aslant. We go into weightless days, seconds, millennia. On the other side of the measure of beats is a time without measure.

We are in a time of dissociation. Not the bad kind, the good kind. We go out of this world. Those thoughts are still here. Those feelings are still here. They don't bother us. This body is still here. We can endure this gendered flesh. We go. We go hard. We're gone.

Then we are back. How long were we out of this gravity time? I don't care to know. We are thirsty. We are tired. We ache. We take a break. We get water. We eat the chocolate bar we always bring. We find a spot to sit. We make out. We kiss. We sense the heat, the vapor of bodies. We feel the bodies all around, separate yet here. Swirling into this same air, fog and sweat. It's hot. We fan ourselves. We rest.

We go again. We dance again. We're gone again. Into sideways time. We drift away from ourselves, into that other time. We are away with the edgeways tide.

We forget. We have a lot to forget. We have time to forget. We have a world to forget. A world in pain. The whole world has dysphoria. We go out of the world and its crooked seasons. We go to another. We go to the era between one beat and the next. We love techno because the beats come fast, so there's much more of that slanted other time folded in there.

We feel the light changing. Daylight coming. Through a hole in the curtain, we feel a beam of that cursed sun finger us. We dance some more and then stop. We find jackets. We are out walking the streets of Brooklyn. We are in this big sky. We have electric skin.

We are back now. We close the curtains. We drink water. Eat raspberries and pistachios. We shed rave clothes. Those sweated rags. We don't shower. We lie in bed. We touch. We play ambient music. We go into ambient time.

We are in the air of this little room, lit with candles and fairy lights. There's art on the walls, by our friends. There's books

on the shelves, by our friends. There's sound in the air, by our friends. They can't see us or hear us or read us. It's a different kind of rave. We don't have much time. We go into this turn, ooze into its calling. We are here. We are healing. We are home.

◆

Jenny, I wrote this for you, and you write back: *We are here, we are healing, we are home—this strikes me as a tender, but weighted statement. I want to feel it. I monitor the together and apart of us. How much of myself is it safe to put here, outside the bed and the dance floor? I want a love that is home. That's what love means to me, here at the end of the world. Here in the middle of my life. A home that will be there tomorrow. Even if it isn't, I'm allowed to believe it.*

We both have avoidance tactics. I've not felt safe to be vulnerable for a long time. And underneath even that, I'm still that sad, frightened little kid. Maybe home is where we don't have to pretend that we're not scarred by life. Where we don't have to keep nursing the wounded part on our own, holding it away from each other. Thinking of you and me and us and that Ethel Cain song: I know it's real when you call me home.

I met you on Tinder. Two years after Christen and I separated, and I moved out. I was living in Brooklyn most of the week, with a roommate. I felt free, but lonely—needing company, emotional or sexual. Flipping through dating apps, not getting matches. I erase my profiles and start over, shaving my age down from fifty-nine to forty-nine. (I passed for it.) Get matches.

Tinder misadventures: when I say I'm trans, they say it's OK because they are into kink. (Then ghost me.) They say they have several selves, only one of them female. (They all need a bath.) They need me to prove I wasn't male-socialized. (I was and was good at it.) They scream when I gently squeeze a tit. (Not on hormones as long as claimed.) They declare they are neither romantically nor sexually attracted to me. (But want to fuck me anyway.) They want to fuck me out of curiosity because they've

read my books. (Or maybe just heard of them.) They admit later they swiped right by accident. (But were charmed by my texting.) And then there's those gentlemen who send dick pics …

When we match, I'm not hopeful. We have writing and books in common, so I propose a walking tour of Lower East Side bookstores. It's a date.

There's a bookstore that sells pickles, and you buy pickles. You open the jar on the street as soon as we step out, to taste them right away. That's the moment I feel. This simple act of claiming a pleasure. A glimpse of capacity for delight. I don't know when you felt you wanted me.

"You're the kind of girl love always finds," says my friend Pet. Maybe, but I so nearly fucked it up from the start. Lying about my age on Tinder, then not owning up to it. You caught me out in the most stupid way: I put my sixtieth birthday party on Insta. To which I hadn't invited you. I'm lucky you were willing to persist with me. I've tried ever since to be as honest as is humanly possible, given that humans are animals that deceive firstly themselves.

It's been more than a year now. Still going. I can't tell the story of us, as it's not a story; it's a spiral, a situation, a rave.

We go looking for the rave most weekends. We're in our heads a lot. We're that kind. We figured out how to make our weird brains work for us. New York is full of people like us. The ruling class needs us to keep spitting out our little twists on the common stock of information. Our weird brains are for sale. We get paid well enough for our weird brain labor. That's how we pay these exorbitant rents. We need to be near other weirdos. Twisting together, in this city, or at least parts of it, where weirdness is common as breath.

We're in our heads a lot so need to get back into our bodies. We dance. Not just dance—we rave. Look around this dance floor: it's weird brain workers, service workers, sex workers. We're all dancing to the point where selves get lost.

◆

I don't want to say too much about you. Here's just one detail I'll share. That you feed the stray cats on your block. That you took them inside during a storm but set them free again. That you want them to live, but to live cat lives.

I've said, I'll say: I love you. We get to make up what that storied word means. The love that's later in life. The love that's queer-for-trans. The love across a twenty-year age gap. The love when a world is ending. I love you like breath, with the certainty with which the next breath comes. With the likelihood that my last breath comes long before yours.

"My biggest fear is that for you this isn't serious, not like all the lovers who you've loved before. Time turns around the sun of your marriage and I'm simply there now that you're lonely when the sun goes down."

We've both loved and been loved before. Maybe I was never much good at it, but I try. I'm in love with you. What comes into that, from the past, is what I've tried to learn. We're not Romeo and Juliet, or even Juliet and Juliet. That myth. Can we live with the possibility that a love that is not innocent, not the hetero couple, not a privatizing turning away from the world —can be not less but far more? Can it be a home both just for us and also in the world? Let's be home.

And then also: Can a transsexual love and be loved? That was a real question for me when I came out, when my marriage ended. The answer of course is yes, or rather, answers. There's more than one kind of transsexual. And kind of love.

My friend Eva talks about what it's like to be born dead. I wasn't that kind of transsexual. I was the kind that could hide it, distract it, divert it. To the point where I became another. I was the kind that could act in the world as if there was ongoingness. I was the kind that lived in the future. I was modern. There was a better world to build for generations to come. I wasn't the born-dead kind, for whom being present in any given moment is an astonishing thing, invested with intensities.

Spatial dysphoria: it feels like my body is wrong, but maybe my body is fine and the world is wrong about it. Maybe this world doesn't allow for the way these sorts of bodies are in space.

Temporal dysphoria: this time is wrong. The dysphoric time that trans women feel. Bodies that don't go through the generic story arc of a cis woman's body. How they lord that over us! Even those that say they're our friends. It's so painful, to be stuck in a body of time that is all so wrong. They've no need to remind us.

You never made me feel that. Even unconsciously you've spared me that. How special that is. How it lets me breathe. How it lets me let you hold me.

You hold my hand through the crowd at the abortion-rights demo. You, who never wanted kids but could get pregnant; me, who wanted to get pregnant but never could. Who became a father and became a woman.

You grab my hand on the dance floor and pull me away from that man I smacked in the face. He was pressing himself against me and others, his dick out, a jacket over his arm to hide it. Sometimes I need you to protect me. With your height, your strength. With your footing in the cis world and your arms long enough to embrace your own queerness as well as— whatever my deal is.

I wouldn't say that being trans now is living my truth. I'd say it's a better fiction. This is the genre of this body now. This is how it breathes easy. It's telling that transsexuals are required to declare we're in possession of true being to transition—a demand not made of other sorts of body. Memoir, the confessed account of the true self, is demanded of us. Fuck that.

I still feel the need to explain myself to you, even though you never ask for that. I was her, was this body feeling itself, as it might want, shorn of the fuzz of masculinity that the world kept insisting was its birthright—when I got fucked hard. The everyday dysphoria was vague and diffuse, but the euphoria in that moment had an unavoidable clarity. That sharp, bright breath.

I felt it too, sometimes, while dancing.

These threads lead into a labyrinth called the sex of the body. Few enter, and those, blindly. So many turns, so many ways to lose the strand, get stranded, or eaten alive, but there's also ways to get through. Not everyone comes out the other side. I came out a transsexual woman. Some come out as other configurations or go back out the way they came. The sex of the body is a hairball of possibilities. All I can write about is this one.

This body—I hacked it. Castration: the psychoanalysts think the problem with transsexual women is that we take it too literally, but the way I see it is that they take it too metaphorically. Unlike them, I speak from experience. A girl really can just cut her nuts off, as the Galli—priestesses of the goddess Cybele—did in ancient times. The cure is ancient and modern—and not just talk.

Jenny, it's work to not feel jealous. I've managed what is in part an approximation of a cis woman's body, but I don't want to be an imitation. With the tech on hand, I made a body that's something else. My way of living with the difference is to be in this flesh as its own work of art. Politically, "trans women are women." But aesthetically, I'm with the t-girls who embrace our difference. Who turn the bad feelings around, revel in our fallen state, become pretty in our own ways.

Maybe cis women and trans women could get along better if we could all admit that we can get jealous of each other's bodies. Some of the most perfect approximations of the Ideal Woman who torments us all are trans: tall, lean, slim hipped—and never get the cramps. It seems infuriating to some that trans women are born with dicks, with all the power they supposedly embody, and don't much care for any of it. The trans woman bears the burden of the absurdity of gender. She is the scapegoat for what everyone imagines they're denied.

Sometimes it feels like you have less unconscious transmisogyny than I do. Maybe it's because you're one of those rare not-trans people who made their own transit through the maze of the body but didn't need the crossing. Your body was the scene of a different kind of struggle, has different scars. Our bodies feel this in each other. Our bodies mother this in each other. Hush now. Don't cry.

When we fuck, our bodies gossip together. So much being alive, be breathing flesh. I don't feel that gender euphoria anymore. Now I don't even miss it. We forget our wounds, the scars of nervous selfhood. We write on and in raveled sheets of skin.

With this hacked body, with you, there's this other writing. This other language I can't translate, liquid soundings. You invoke God a lot when you cum. To me it's our goddess Cybele, she with her drum, her philter and her lions. Goddess of ravers, stoners, trannies—and cat ladies.

We joke that there's no pride flag for sexual people who are just into other sexual people, who don't care all that much about categories and identities. I imagine that flag would just be a transparent rectangle. Clear plastic refracting diamond light.

Our lives now have a part that is in each other. Whatever I think or feel, you are part of what might think or feel it. Part of you is just here. As Rimbaud almost said: I is in-other. I feel you in this noisy stream of sensations that sounds in the empty warehouse of the self. Wherever I go a little of you comes too. We go. This "we" is not the Roomba of the cis-het couple. It's a different dance. Maybe better for some. For us.

When I was young, I thought love was like a Shelley poem, that "we shall become the same, we shall be one." Now that just makes me think of those cis-het couples who speak to each other as "we." As in: "We are sending little Jason to private school." Or, "We are going to renovate the kitchen." I want a "we" with our differences still in it. Not just mine from you, but the other others each of us also are.

◆

It wasn't the first time I'd made you mad, but it was the first time you made me cry. Walking through the fall leaves in the park, by the Hudson, listening to you say what's on your mind and in your heart, and I say, "Look at that bird!" A pretty bird I'd never seen before. You felt slighted. Angry with me, you took off at a cracking pace.

I can't keep up. I'm lagging. You stop and wait for me, breathless, catching up. We're in a parking lot. It takes a moment, as always, before you tell me how you feel. About how you opened up to me and I didn't listen. I say I'm sorry. That's when I'm crying. You hold me there as I need to be held.

It felt like you were leaving me behind. I don't know why this hit so hard. There's no memory to dredge, so I can only imagine. Maybe it was my mother or my sister walking too fast for my little legs. The feeling that what I did or said was so wrong I'll be left forever.

Oh, we're in each other now, deep and cold. We can hurt each other. There were twists in our courses toward this conjoining. We're bent by everything that pushed against our ebb. Mixed tidings eddy in the current where we meet. I'm trying, with all I gathered along the way, to merge with you.

I write because I love the world, and its pain. And you are in the world. I feel the world through you and you through the world. Neither of us can open ourselves to others, to the world, so easily. I want more than anything to open my scarred heart to you. It's been hurt, but still there's beats.

When you write with the people in your life, there's no alibis. Writing becomes praxis. Sometimes I think writing is all I can do at all well. I'm still learning how to love and be loved.

◆

We go to sleep early, to get up early, to go to the rave. It's 4:00 a.m. We eat light, get caffeine in our bodies. Take psilocybin. Pick outfits. We wear light jackets. It's fall, not cold yet. We pack rave bags. Check for the location. Call a car. Rainy night, the sky a gray hoodie.

How did we get here? Among these swerving particles. We

are on a picket of time where there's still time. We go into freightless days, seconds, millennia. On the other side of the pleasure of beats is a time without ledger.

We forget. We have a lot to forget. We go out of the world and its wonky seasons. We go to the era between one breath and the next. We dance some more and then stop. We don't have much time. We go into this turn, seep into its calling. We are here. We are healing. We are home.

Others

(To Veronica)

You can be such a bitch, Veronica. It was supposed to be just a friendly lunchtime conversation. Just two trans women, at home in each other's company in a hostile world. Instead, you picked a fight.

Sure, the "personal is political," but the political can also get very personal—particularly in your mouth. Not to mention your subtweets. Rather than engage in that discourse, I'm sending you this version of how the conversation could have gone.

We're at lunch in a Manhattan restaurant. Everyone around us looks like they work in the information trades. There's a couple of suited bros peering at a spreadsheet on a laptop. Everyone else is casually fashionable. Even the straight-acting cis men sport signature eyewear. All the patrons are white—or white-acting.

As are we, Veronica. We fit right in. We have steady jobs in the information trades. We're dressed professionally, but no suits for us—we're not management. We're creative sorts. But not *too* creative.

Service is slow, and we've both downed our first cocktail, so we play the Crisp Game. I learned it from a brief encounter with the legendary Quentin Crisp, failed sex worker turned writer. To play, we read the other patrons and tell each other stories about which of them has been fucked in the ass.

"The first one's too easy! That one's a chaser, already gave me the eye. Chaser who wants a trans girl to pop a dick-pill to fuck him. And won't pay for it."

"That one is getting pegged on the regular by a cis woman—not his wife."

"That one, well, gay bottom. Obvious. We know, honey, we know!"

"That one, but he only did it in college."

"That one puts out for her boyfriend, but she doesn't like it."

"T-girl bottom wisdom: never let anyone fuck you in the ass who has not themselves been fucked in the ass—and enjoyed it."

"You should tweet that."

So it goes, until our food arrives.

This game is also a reminder. Nobody is what they appear. Well, of the two of us, I'm the easily clockable kind. You are so much closer to the model of feminine beauty. Have to be, to keep gender dysphoria from ruining your life.

As with most trans women, our internalized transphobia means we have appraised each other from the point of view of some ideal model of feminine form. Everything I can see about you is beauty, but the one thing I know that you feel doesn't pass is your hands. You wear no rings, have clear lacquered nails. My nails are purple with sparkles. My hands are about the only thing that does pass.

Our friendship: I want to be seen in public with you because of your elegance. You will be seen with me even though it means that because of me you'll get clocked. This generosity affirms your strength of character, which is gratifying in itself, and is a gift to me, the awkward stepsister.

Not much is going to happen to us, today at least, even if the cis sniff us out. Privilege lets us do this—particularly as white New Yorkers with excellent manners.

We talk about this. "I've still been called a trap," you say.

"Me too. And this is what's strange: even such an obvious trans woman as me gets called a trap. The cis think the essence of our being is nothing more than a failure to deceive them."

"If trans women are traps, it's because everyone is," you contend.

"Oh really? How do you arrive at that?"

"Nobody is ever quite what they appear. Take the Crisp Game we just played. Our surmises could be wildly off."

"It's more fun that way," I interject.

"But there's always *something*. Maybe suit-guy over there," you gesture with your clockable hand, "isn't getting pegged—but instead has a stash of shemale porn."

"There's always a gap between the representation and what it presents. That's how all communication works," I declare.

"What do you mean?" Well, you asked for it. We're going to play the Theory Game. You order more drinks.

"There's always a difference between the sign of the thing and the thing itself. How I appear isn't all of me. Perception always has an element of deception."

"There's something irksome, but also delicious, about that," you say, with a glinting eye.

I guess where your saucy bent will take this game, but I'm in a more philosophical mood. "Judging by their appearances, all the patrons in this restaurant look like they work with signs and do pretty well at it. Everyone looks prosperous, successful, capable. It's unlikely that they all are."

"That girl's shoes, for example," you tilt your hand to guide my eye again. Cracked leather, worn heel.

I can play this game too. "That one over there, leaning in, a bit too overeager—is asking for money." Not everyone is here, as we are, at leisure. There's a lot of hustling going on.

"Everyone is always concealing something," you say.

"We're always differing from the signs we make. It might be a specifically Western-culture kind of hang-up, but there's a nervousness about this gap between sign and thing."

"Which is why they," you gesture at the cis around us, "want to stick it to trans women—as traps."

"In Plato's philosophy"—I'm getting pretentious, but you like it when I play the Theory Game, and it will seduce you away from what I'm not telling you about my life—"it's not just that the sign of the thing falls short of the thing itself. The thing itself also falls short, in turn, of the pure idea or form of the thing. Behind appearances are things. But things, too, are just a kind of mere appearance: behind things are their forms. These cannot be touched, or tasted, or seen. They are knowable only to thought itself."

"But who cares about Plato?" You dismiss him with a wave.

"Nietzsche called Christianity 'Platonism for the masses.' In Christianity, too, appearances are suspect—are now the work of the devil. Actual things are not to be trusted either, particularly if those things are bodies. These are corrupt flesh, condemned to die. What is real is something, once again, invisible, untouchable—pure spirit. If spirit refuses to be corrupted by appearances or by the pleasures of the flesh, it can join God in eternity."

"So, have you been having any pleasure of the flesh lately— *with anyone I know?*" You are on to me. I'd better try to hold your attention by throwing a conversational curveball.

"Secular Western culture inherited a residue of Platonism via Christianity. Even some kinds of Marxists imagine a world of false appearances. For them, it's capitalism. The overthrow of capitalism restores 'man' to the possibility of an authentic life: no more advertising, good riddance to fashion, and bye-bye to alienation. Man is restored to himself as himself."

"Men. Hmph. I don't know what anyone sees in them." You're trying to quit them and go dyke like me. With, shall we say, mixed results. I've distracted you from the distraction. I'll have to get us back on track.

"I said 'man' here intentionally, because what these Marxists find suspect has a certain femininity to it. They associate femininity with the world of commodities. Femininity, as a handful of signs for sex, beauty and youth, is understood only as something deployed deceptively to sell products."

"It's hard to be soft, to be femme. Men think there's nothing firm there, that they can just push us around." This, I know, is a subject upon which you've made yourself an authority, one from which I've much to learn.

"In all these versions of Platonism, it's the *femme* that's most suspect, where femme might stand for all the signs and attributes of femininity that point to their bearer being a woman. To have started life with 'MALE' stamped on our birth certificates, to transition at some point outside of masculinity—is then extra suspect. The femme is that which deceives, but 'woman,' ironically enough, in all these Western discourses, deceives about everything *but itself*."

"You say I deceive about everything but myself?" You pretend to be offended, but I can see from that little smile that you like this.

"Femme signs supposedly deceive about a lot of things, but not about the womanhood of those who produce such signs."

"Nobody accuses a feminine cis woman of not being a woman," you add, crossly. The gap between them and you is a sensitive subject. I think before I speak, but I want to press you a little further. "This is what is different about the figure of the transsexual woman in this Platonist universe. It is not a femininity deceiving about something else. It is deceptive *about femininity*. In trap metaphysics, you and I are a special kind of deceiver."

"So we're not women who as women are deceivers; we are deceivers about being women. Sort of like double deceivers. Super-femmes!" You crack us both up.

"Precisely. You see, previously there was what's true, which is Plato's 'idea,' and two fallen states, which are the thing and then—even more fallen—the representation. The idea embodies truth for the Platonist. God and communism do it for Christians and Marxists. What is true is identical to itself. It allows no gap between itself and any aspect of itself. It is incapable of making a mere sign of itself. It is pure—and unrepresentable."

You get your faraway look, and say, to the air more than to me: "Sometimes I feel like the woman I'm trying to be is an impossible idea. That no matter how much I try to be her, already am her anyway, the farther away it seems. I think it hurts us, your Platonist idea of woman—and not just us. All those cis feminists who hate us struggle with her too."

"Yes!" I hadn't thought of this part. "They have to hate us as bad simulation of the idea of 'woman' so they don't have to deal with their own failure as representatives of that idea."

"It's a hierarchy, from most to least, where we're always at the bottom." I can see that look of yours that signals a low mood. I have to get on to the crux of this argument. The part, for us, that invokes a T4T world of possibility.

I launch another move: "OK, so this is also how a certain brand of feminism thinks about the figure of woman. That she just *is*. There's hand waving about biological chromosomes, but those are things that are outside the everyday realm of human perception. Woman is a Platonic ideal that 'real' women just embody by default as variations upon perfection. They then inevitably join misogynists in their distrust of femme signs as deception, and the trap as the lowest deceiver of all."

"That's fucked up," you declare.

"Agreed. In this Platonic world, no sensible thing can do justice to the pure realm of the true. No readable representation can do justice even to things, let alone to the pure and true idea. Instead, appearances are seducing you: away from philosophy in Plato, away from God in Christianity, away from the Revolution in Marxism, away from the essence of Woman in feminism. In all cases, these appearances get coded all too often as femme. Femme lacks reason, faith, revolutionary fidelity."

"Or, oddly enough, feminists who claim such Platonic big-dick energy by holding the line against traps."

"Yes. Femme signs are suspect, but not suspected of pointing to their bearer being anything other than a woman. Then: along comes you and me. We've fallen even below the most fallen. We are as far as you can get from the pure idea."

"We're all in the gutter, but some of us are fallen stars!"

"We are far from even the imperfect embodiment of the idea in a thing. We are not the even more imperfect embodiment of the thing or idea in a representation. In this metaphysics, you are not even that which truly makes deceptive signs with your femininity. You are *deceptively* making deceptive signs—as a trap."

"Fuck you too, hun."

"Hear me out, babe. You at least get to be a trap. *I'm not even that.* I am the figure who *fails* to make the deceptive signs of womanhood, a comical failure. You are the trap who succeeds, who is a dangerous deceiver. The Platonic order of things makes me the failed version of you, while you are the failed version of the cis body, who is the failed version of the ideal."

"I don't want to be on the bottom—just because I am a bottom."

"It's such a temptation among trans women to rank ourselves against each other. You are my friend and dear to me because you refuse that. We both know what I am. I'm a brick. But you wouldn't call me that. Not to my face, at least."

"I would *never* call you that!" You touch my hand. I'm going to cry.

"I don't care that I'm a brick. A lump of burnt dirt formed into shape—with feet of clay, women's size nine." Runway model size, handy for shopping at sample sales. I'm suddenly aware that you're as sensitive about your big feet as your hands. I didn't mean to be catty. "Anyway, the only difference between us is the threshold of possible discovery. My picture on a dating app fools nobody. That chaser guy over there," I wave a slender finger, "giving me the eye knows I'm a tranny and is hoping there's girldick under this Gogo Graham skirt."

"Well, he's got that right."

"Whereas you have found yourself in dangerous situations, particularly with men who are interested in you before they clock you, or before you decide—or not—to disclose." I touch your hand now. I know those stories. I know this is hard. "There are special punishments for the trap. If they want to fuck us, declare their desire, and only then find out we're a trap—they can kill us. We fall that low in the ranks that approximate the true."

"We're disposable. Not even things. Trash to them," your carefully coached voice cracks with restrained rage. We hold hands for a moment. Make eye contact. Look away.

A wave of feeling too intense to acknowledge passes over us. When it abates, I take up the conversational play again. "There's something inherently conservative in all these versions of what we might rather casually label trap metaphysics. Who decides on what is closest or furthest from the pure and true?"

"Not your transsexual ass, or mine!" You say it a little too loudly, a little too drunkenly, and not quite with your girl voice.

"This is why the Crisp Game is so delicious. We turn the cis gaze back on itself."

Your mood brightens a little: "I just like to play it with you for shits and giggles."

"Suit guy thinks he gets to pass judgment on us. And he did, with that classic glance-and-glare. The glance is attracted by something: maybe my long, straight, bare thigh. Maybe your gorgeous tits."

"I do have gorgeous tits …" Looking at them, I concede this with a smile. I know where they stop and padding fills in the rest, from that time I took your bra off at that party—but we never talk about that.

I pick up the thread again: "But then suit guy clocks me, and we get the glare. It says: *You wasted a second of my life in which I might have eye-banged you, and you turn out to be nothing but a filthy transsexual, whose sight disgusts me. Or worse: attracts and disgusts me.* We play our little game as we know that everyone has secrets."

You fill in the line of thought for me. "Everyone is a trap; nobody's gaze is authoritative. Not even that suit guy."

"To be a transsexual woman is to be the scapegoat of an

order of representation in which someone has to be held accountable for the failure of signs to be adequate to things. In trap metaphysics, we're comprehensible only as the lowest kind of deceivers. To the cis, we are *choosing* to be female. But who would *choose* that? So we must be traps, deceivers. We are the *even-worse* things in the world."

"Cheers to that!" Deciding we're to get hammered, you order another round.

"Compared to most of our sort, we hold on to a few privileges, you and I. Since no one dares to use the word 'class,' let's use polite words: 'socioeconomic status.' Your tech job and my teaching job will pay for our talents, and we can walk into a restaurant where the servers will assume that our credit cards at least are valid—"

"You're getting the check, right?"

"—and yet we are still seen as a lesser kind of being by many of these other diners around us—including some who would patronize us with the muggy embrace of their liberal acceptance. They feel like they stand in the position of authority, as representatives of the idea of gender, gifting us our humanity."

"Fuck that!"

"Fuck that!" I raise my glass to yours. Clink. "There's something suspect about taking intangible ideal forms of anything as the most real, including ideas of gender. I'd rather delight in the tangible play of appearances than buy into this whole hierarchy of truth and being. Nietzsche was wrong about more than a few things, but—becoming woman, as he only wrote, as we achieve, is to escape the hierarchy of the true and the false."

"To do otherwise is just boring," you say. "It's to just take the order of things for granted."

"Seeing appearances as the shortcomings of a prior state of true being is indeed boring, I agree." Warmed by the drinks, I'm warming to my theme. "Let's work the surfaces, change the signs, fashion the possibility of being to come! We are not fallen imitations of cisters. We add fresh edits to the flesh, with the latest techniques, the latest information, in all fields. We are an avant-garde of flesh! What if a world existed that could answer to the call of our bodies?"

"I want to live in that world."

I'm drunk and on a roll: "Maybe that's utopian. In the meantime, girls like us pursue an irrepressible need to transition, to bend information and technique to finding forms in which we might abide. Maybe that's another reason we become scapegoats. We make ourselves over, in the here and now, as bodies, not ideas. And we do it together. We make our own home world, tenuous and compromised and fractious as it is—inside and yet apart from the cis world. They think they know our little secret, but we have information about being that they will never know."

"Speaking of secrets, didn't I see you leave the rave with my nemesis this morning? What the fuck?" I was hoping to distract you from that. Alright, so I fucked your ex and didn't tell you. These things happen, hun. The heart, or rather the ass, wants what it wants.

"Our secret is that there isn't one," I venture. "We don't know anything about the true, hidden nature of gender, and neither do the cis. All trans girls have is the evidence of our dysphoric senses and a will to create a femininity with which to live. And it's better if we do it together."

"Your whole theory is to explain to yourself why you think trans girls are hot."

"Maybe," I concede. "But it could be something else as well. Maybe what I'm talking about is our *femmunism*."

"Our what?"

"Our femmunism. Not communism, premised on a truth to come once the false, alienated commodified world is overthrown. Our femmunism: a world of actual appearances, in the here and now, signaling possibilities to each other. A T4T that's not all fucks and fights and inevitable disappointments. That's made together knowing only that we have nothing in common. That the nothing is what's common—or what's *femmon*, rather."

"You lost me there, but I like it."

"The common, the community, communication, communism, all derive from the *munus*, which to the Romans was both a gift and a burden, a favor and an obligation, both public works and spectacle. Rather than what's *co-munus*, that which is shared as if it was universal, I'm talking about what's *fe-munus*, just between us. Not the abstract, timeless public sphere that is supposedly for all but really just for cis white men."

"Oh, I see what you did: you're saying the liberal notion of the ideal public sphere and its model speech acts is also a Platonist universal masking the particulars of a commonality that excludes us."

"You caught me out. Instead of which a femmunism without governing ideals, that is sensual, actual, particular."

"Kiki as praxis," you say, in an almost dreamy tone.

"Ironically, it makes us the best thing in the world. The trans woman as the femme who is the false maker of the false. Truth as a woman. We are those whose unbidden desires make everything. And to the extent that everyone turns their desires into signs of something other than an approximation to a non-existent ideal, not only is everyone femme; everyone is trans. Only difference is that we know it. We're ahead of the game!"

"You're so pretty when you go off like that," you tease.

"'Pretty' is an interesting word. The pretty is different to the beautiful."

"If you're fishing for compliments, I can say you look beautiful."

"I'm not fishing, and I'm not fish, but I like to be pretty. Pretty, not beautiful. It's not that the pretty is different to the beautiful in degree, as if it was further from an ideal, had lesser being. It's different in kind."

"Aha! Platonism again! It's like your game today is to show everything has the same trap metaphysics. Where there's a form or idea, that's what's really true, and everything falls short of it by degrees."

"You twigged to my little game," I concede. "But let me put in a word for this other way of being in the world, and why trans girls are already doing it, and know it—whether we *know* we know it or not."

"Do tell."

"The word 'pretty' comes from words that suggested the brisk, the clever, the tricky. Over centuries it became connected to femininity, to smallness, weakness, getting by on wits and wiles. Being crafty and crafting appearances. Where beauty clads the pure form it approximates, the pretty can be a bit of a ruse, a decoy. The pretty is suspect in an era of commodity culture. It hides a defect."

"The defect that we're traps. That while we can be bred, we can't breed. No wombs." You gesture to your own delightfully curved belly.

"We're traps for male desire. The ideal of Woman we supposedly fake is a reproductive one. Platonist metaphysics is all about paternity. Copies are judged as more or less proximate progeny of a timeless idea. The illegitimate copy, transposed in from elsewhere, has to be detected and rejected. Fuck that, though. What if what was pretty could lead desire astray in more interesting ways. Out of the reproduction of boredom. Toward forms of being that are no longer copies of an impossible, nonexistent original. Which are rather variations upon variations, a femmunism of experimental forms, whose existence attains being only in relation to each other. Let the sensuous tell us what is, and what's possible. Well, that could be us, babe. That could be trans women. That could be our T4T world."

"What about trans men?"

"I don't know, hun. I leave it up to them to create their own T4T utopia. I expect you'll find it if they do."

"What about nonbinaries?"

"A nonbinary utopia is neither here nor there."

"Don't tweet that."

"A nonbinary undoing of the Platonic metaphysics of the hierarchy of being would be different again. We can each have our own critique of the universality of Platonist metaphysics and our own particular universal alternative. Made in their here and now, out of whatever practice emerges out of the difference between our own being with each other and the world that denies that being."

"So your little game is that for trans women, we take the idea that we are traps and turn it inside out, to make not being a proper cis copy of some impossible ideal a positive value. What about cis women?"

"We are living proof that it's possible to be women without reference to the reproduction of an ideal of Woman. I think a lot of cis women want that too, even though they resist the possibilities we embody. But I am, in a sneaky way, making us trans women not an ideal at all, but more like a possible avant-garde of another kind of femininity when we make our being together with reference only to each other.

"Speaking of trans women: I *saw* you leave the rave with her last night, and you know she's tried to cancel me. What the *fuck*, honey?"

I catch the server's eye and hastily gather the check.

(To Venus)

For a long time, I harbored a secret name. I was Ken or Kenneth to the world, but to myself I was another. To the point where she almost calved off as a separate personality.

That name was Karen. A name that belonged to a classmate from high school, a popular girl, whom of course I wanted to be or be like.

On a school excursion we all went horse riding. As the best rider, Karen rode the best horse. On the home stretch, the horse bolted. She lost control. We all heard her screams. Thrown to the ground, into a coma from which she never arose.

I know. There's something fucked-up about taking her name.

Much later, the name Karen became a meme: the generic name of the generic white woman who calls the cops to complain about Black people. I gave up on changing my government name to Karen. Or to anything. Just speaking for myself: I don't care about my government name or gender.

Ironically, that I have the luxury of not caring about my government name or gender, that I never legally became Karen—is peak Karen.

What I feel called to work on is that I am a Karen, or at least that any claim I might make to womanhood means a reckoning with myself as a Karen—a white woman. A sentiment I expressed to you more than once. To which you gave your gentlest eye roll.

◆

When we met, we both still went by our government names, and genders. You had certain skills of observation and saw something I barely saw myself: that we shared a secret. That we were both girls. You were the only person other than Christen who knew my other name. It came out in an exchange of confidences. After you read the Karen in me.

Your secret name was Venus, partly after Venus Williams, whom you resembled. More after something Saidiya Hartman wrote, about the Black women aboard the slave ships, about whom the archive says so little, and most of that recording only their disposition as property. Sometimes their enslavers called them Venus. Like Hartman you wanted to fabulate stories about Black women's lives, to make them matter, only you wanted to write stories for the women about whom Hartman hadn't had much to say: Black trans women.

You taught me things about transsexuality. What I thought was my private secret was a shared secret, a covert commons. I'm in on it now.

I wasn't ready to come out. You were past ready, but the world was against you. When you stepped out into the world as Venus, it cost you dear. There was no hiding your Blackness, which already marked you for trouble. When you came out, that was then multiplied by your estrangement from your religious family, and by poverty, precarity, by being far from a home that wasn't even home anymore.

You wanted a teacher for the one thing you thought I might know: about writing, an art you saw as controlled by white people—which it has to be said is an accurate read. I offered edits, gave notes, some advice. Encouraged you to submit your writing, which I don't think you ever did. "Submit" is a loaded word here when considering the Black writer and a world of white editors and gatekeepers, including me.

After I came out and started to go out, I'd see you at raves. Sometimes I'd rather not be recognized as Professor Wark as I'm off the clock, but with you I didn't mind. I'll never forget the gabba show where I talked you through writing your book proposal, shouting through the ultrafast beats and pulsing lights.

I couldn't help but hope you'd pitch it, but part of me knew it would never happen. You didn't lack for talent or resolve. It's that sliver of self-doubt on top of all the material obstacles. Living in that garage, coping with the stress of sex work. I wanted to believe you could still write, like you wanted.

I don't care if it's naive, but I believe everyone can make art. Maybe not everyone is the next Saidiya Hartman or Janet Mock, but everyone can make art that means something in their lives and the lives of those around them. But then, I've led a luxury life. The world left a little clearing where that was achievable for me. A clearing called whiteness.

Not for you. The money you could make was good enough, but it was cash. Cash from dealing, cash from sex work. Sometimes dangerous, and when not dangerous, emotionally fraught. Housing became a problem. Hard to rent when you have no digital money trail.

It got worse. Chronic, low-level health problems, salved with street meds. And then you became known to the police. You saw where things were heading. Trying to get by on legit jobs, but with no résumé, making minimum wage. The hormones reshaping your face, pushing out tits, making boymode physically as well as emotionally impossible.

You taught me a concept for all this: *transmisogynoir*. The hatred of Black trans femininity, that most fallen thing. You taught me more than I taught you. Which merely extends and reinforces the structure within which you struggled and in which I was mostly left untouched.

Let's not let pass without mention, let's not have slip into nothingness, the times I got to be in your presence when you got free. On the dance floor, eyes closed, that serpentine writhe, that curlicue of the hand, raised over your head. That smile. The way you could just release yourself into movement in the summer heat. The memory of that is sacred to me.

Then fall, and the COVID lockdown. I lost touch. You weren't answering my texts. You kept me separate from the rest of your world as you knew you didn't fit in mine. Then summer again, a cool summer compared to those to come, but the mood in the streets—fire.

An unexpected text from you, to make sure I'll come. To the uprising for Black lives. I came, just a body among others, there because you called. Meaning you, Venus, and you, that to which you belonged—Black life. Out on the streets of Brooklyn, after curfew, me in one little group, running into you in another.

"What's the vibe?" I asked.

You smiled, wide enough to crack the world. "A Black rave."

Joining forces. Off to find others. Our streets! You were brave; I was timid. I tried to warm myself on your courage, which part of me also felt as reckless. As if your life didn't matter.

I came to listen, to witness, to refuse to be governed. Refusing the order of violence that divides us, that inflicts pain on you beyond even the reasons of order and property. I'm not telling you anything you don't know. I'm just repeating the lesson back, responding to the call. To be on the same page.

I gave up one thing that put me on the side of those who get to enjoy at a distance the prospect of violence against an-other. I gave up masculinity. This wasn't for political reasons, or even for reasons. Now everywhere I go, no matter what they think of me, people get to deal with someone who does not appear in the guise of a man. I'd give up whiteness, but that's different. What you taught me is it's mine whether I want it or not.

◆

A story I never told you: rewind back to summer 2019. I'm in Times Square. Tourists clot the sidewalk. I'm lost, which is embarrassing for a New Yorker. I'm heading up Seventh Avenue. I'm aware this whole time that I'm with my ten-year-old child. We are going to Flame Con, the queer comics convention at the Sheraton Hotel.

I see three young Black men on the sidewalk. They are giving away free CDs. One is pressing a CD into my hand. I know this hustle. Once it's in my hand, he will ask for ten dollars. So I don't take it. He's persistent.

"Ma'am, ma'am, ma'am," he says.

"No thank you."

"Ma'am."

"No thank you."

"Ma'am."

"Fuck off."

"Hey," says one of the others, "that's a dude."

"That's a dude!" The third chimes in.

"Fuck off."

Now all three of them are following me up the street, taunting.

"Suck my dick!" All of them start on this one.

"Suck my dick!" Their tone shifts toward menace.

I'm walking faster, but they still follow. That won't work. I turn around and face them, making sure my child is behind me, a bitch shielding her cub. It's a standoff. Heart pounding techno tempo. Seconds stretch out so long you can look around inside them. I'm aware of where we are. There's surveillance cameras everywhere—and probably cops.

That's when I ask myself: if the cops arrive, are they more likely to take the side of three Black men, or my white tranny faggot ass? And I think it'd be me. That if this gets ugly and the cops show, whiteness will protect me. Conflicting feelings: none of my encounters with cops have ever been pleasant, but "unpleasant" has been the worst of it. I want to be safe, but I don't want police to be what saves me.

Looking around, inside the second it takes to think tactics, for a way out. Now they're chanting: "Suck my dick! Suck my dick!" I hold up both hands and point to my tranny self. "No! You come here and *suck mine*!" A beat—one of those where time bungees down forever before it snaps back. Laughter. They're laughing. At me rather than with me. It doesn't matter.

Better to be a pathetic joke than a threat to masculinity. They go back to hustling tourists.

I take my child's hand and, looking around, spot the lobby of another hotel. Ah, just ducking in here would have been a less risky street tactic. As a well-enough-dressed white person, I can enter any hotel lobby. We sit down and hold each other, which comforts me, at least. Hearts pound. We talk about how not to handle oneself on the street, which turns into a discussion of race, class and transphobia. We hug. "I love you Dad." We go off in search of comics and cosplayers.

◆

I don't know what could be a more basic, gut-level, urgent urge toward revolution than the existence of surplus pain. My mother's premature death was a thing of flesh. Yours, Venus, came from the violence of marginal labor, from the order of the straight family, from antiblackness. Nothing will ever extort a reconciliation from me to any of that. No story where that is wished away will ever hold me happily ever after. Maybe it's why I don't trust stories at all.

I heard through the transsexual grapevine that you had chosen to leave your life. Or maybe: chosen to steal it back from the living death of antiblackness. It was during the lockdown, that time of isolation. The lockdown saved a lot of lives, but it took some as well.

You'd think I'd be inured to loss by now. I bear it like a duty. The coldness where I touch what pushed you toward the limit. The hot rage I feel against what did the pushing.

I went by myself to Green-Wood Cemetery. Found Jean-Michel Basquiat's headstone. I sat on the cool grass for a while, then gathered twigs and made a little altar of them against the nearest tree. The living wood against the dead. As I had when Kato passed. I would have so loved for the two of you to meet, in life. Kneeling before this makeshift shrine, I tried to pour all the frozen sadness in my heart out onto the ground, but I

couldn't. I poured out a little Cointreau, your favorite, from a flask, instead.

◆

The Brooklyn Museum has a sunken forecourt that makes it something of an amphitheater. Christen drove us both here this bright June afternoon to hear leading Black trans women step out of the queer chorus and assume their roles as icons in the movement for Black lives, for the abolition of prisons and police, that whole cadaverous modernity, for the revolution that just has to be made to make these lives livable—and with that, everyone's. We've come for Brooklyn Liberation for Black Trans Lives.

Venus, I felt your shadow standing in the gaps between bodies. How you would have embraced all the feelings of this day. Maybe cracking that grin, hollering with delight, with relief, with rage.

Two more Black trans women died just the week before. Riah Milton (age twenty-five), murdered in Ohio. Dominique "Rem'mie" Fells (age twenty-seven), murdered in Philadelphia. Last May, police shot and killed Tony McDade, a Black trans man (age thirty-eight). Just yesterday, video recorded from outside Layleen Xtravaganza Cubilette-Polanco's cell at Rikers the day she died surfaced, which showed correction officers waited an hour and a half before calling for medical help. Layleen was twenty-seven.

It's a tricky thing: to not lose sight of the dead, to say your names, honor them, and yet not stop there. I say your name quietly: "Venus." What I want to remember is the life that in another world might be yours. That dance floor joy, those brilliant scraps of prose, as more than just fragments. You saw so clearly that what barred your love of the world was the order of the world, and that to love the world this world has to end.

The organizers asked us to wear white. I chose the Ghost slip over the Rick Owens—both of which Christen gave me.

I blend with the human filaments of the crowd, bristling over the grounds all around the museum. Coming up Washington Avenue, I see you assembling, so many overlapping and varying shades of collective Black. Black and trans but also, augmenting your body, queer and cis and white. So many white-clad bodies streaming, milling, chatting, buying ice cream from the truck, clapping and cheering on cue, although from here nothing much can be heard beyond oratorial cadence. Everyone keeps a few feet apart. Everyone wears masks.

We're late. Checking the Signal app on my phone: Jessie gives me her location, but there's no way to get to her without combing through the crowd. The parkway running east-west along the front of the museum is like the languid back of some sleek animal, covered in brilliant fur. Too dense to weave through, so I circle around and amble down Lincoln Place, which runs parallel, one street back. Circling back around to the parkway, there's construction. I pick my way around it. Jessie is by the 2 and 3 train entrance, but I don't see her. Maybe I drifted the wrong way around. Few people, so I'm going in closer. I can almost hear the speakers.

There's a catwalk over the top of the entrance to the museum. I see someone going up there, so I follow. It's not roped off or guarded. Up top I can see the whole western half of the demo. It has a peculiar texture. There's no tight knot at the front. Everyone is keeping their distance.

Ianne Fields Stewart takes the mic. "Black people where y'all at?" The crowd roars back, like lions after slumber. "See that police helicopter? Let's let the militarized police state know exactly how the fuck we feel about them!" Thousands of fingers rise and flip the bird. "For too long, Black trans people have fought for our humanity." Roar!

"Today is the last day!" Stewart leans into her cadence, performing a series of promissory futures, whose possibility teeters on the actions of those here gathered. It isn't really the last day. It could become, with this witnessing, the first day of the possibility of these days ending. Our affirmations—roar!— bid us bind ourselves to it.

Stewart talks about the matter, the materiality, of Black trans lives mattering. "Transphobia ends today." Roar! "And it doesn't end because your nonprofit got a grant off of it. It doesn't end because you put a trans flag on a credit card. It doesn't even end because you said to your white family that trans lives matter. It doesn't end because you fuck us and still misgender us to your friends. Transphobia ends today, because if you ain't with us, you are gonna to learn what it means to be against us!" Roar!

I feel my being exceed itself, expand, exult. Can a performance enacted together communicate the feeling of wants and needs that go beyond even the political, that speak the world where the world is alive?

Ceyenne Doroshow takes the mic. I've met her, at the Body Hack night at Mood Ring. Río introduced us. I didn't have anything to say other than that I was honored. Like the other speakers, she addresses herself mostly to you, making the rest of us spear-carriers in this production. As it should be. "Black trans people send me some love! I love all of you!"

"This is what trans lives look like." Ceyenne gets emotional, her voice cracks. "For every girl that died. The police need to be ashamed of themselves. For every time we had to bury one of ours. They need to be ashamed of themselves. Everyone one of these babies you see behind me. And these babies down here—I want you bitches to *live*!"

The crowd roars. I'm crying. I think of you, Venus. That everyone should be loved. To fall away from some arbitrary ideal of the human is to be excluded from love and included in violence. But then maybe that's not really love, the love that's bounded by violence, bound to violence. Maybe there's another, one you didn't think you'd ever find. We both lost mothers, in such different ways, blistered over loss, in such different ways. Losing kin, fellowship, left too deep a wound. You never found another. And yet here it is today, this other practice of belonging, care, kith. That which would need be centered if there's ever to be a concept of femmunism.

Ceyenne: "Babies, I love you. I love each and every one of my trans family members. I want you to breathe! To stand tall! And proud! And Black!" Roar. "We're whorrrrrrrres!" Roar! "If you could smell me right now. I smell like good pussy!" We're not in church anymore. This is the flip side of that language —its tail. Ceyenne is speaking as, and to, Black trans sex workers. "I gotta tell you, if I didn't tell you, you're looking at a Black international whore baby. It's me. And I'm selling me, to save you."

To Ceyenne, nothing changes unless Black trans people control their own organizations, raise their own money and, most important of all: own their own property. She wants to invest in a material base for Black trans life. Part of my brain wants to read this as a petit bourgeois idea, but then another part of my brain reminds that part that I own property. That I am petit bourgeois already. An inheritance born of white colonial extraction. I'm not battling systematic, racist exclusion.

I think about walking the length of the catwalk to see more of the crowd. Glancing over to the east, I see two people blocking the path. One looks like a tall, Black cis man and the other like a less tall, white cis woman. They have shades on and are blank faced, as if they were acting as security. They *are* security. I'd not noticed that all the orators addressing the crowd are up here.

Each of the speakers up here has the bearing of a goddess. I'm reminded of how for you, not only approximating but exceeding the Platonic ideal of feminine beauty was your armor for survival. Everything conspires to minimize Black trans women. So you, they, sometimes maximize yourselves, become larger than life. It's a femme art not every girl can pull off. It must be exhausting. Were racism and transphobia really to end today, would this style of performing the power of the self end too? Would we still have our icons, our queens?

Craning around security, I see Ceyenne as she steps back from the mic, resplendent in shining black gloves and black cape over a white dress, a bright scarf over her head, under a broad-brimmed black hat.

I see Raquel Willis, in a simple white tee and jeans, a different trans femme style. She takes the mic out of its stand, comes up close to the edge of the railing, looks down at the crowd, letting us breathe. We sip on the image of her drinking us in. I've never met her, but you and I saw her speak at a rally back in summer 2019, just after Layleen died in solitary at Rikers.

I'm thinking of the contrast between that event and this one. That one was downtown, a stone's throw from City Hall. Not that any stones were thrown. The mood was a slow-burning anger, grief, despair—rage. Your Black trans rage. Raquel reminded us that day that the first Pride was a riot, that not much changes without the refusal to be governed. It was, like all good movement oratory, prophetic.

From up on the catwalk, Raquel reminds us of the ancestors, the Black and brown trans women who are the uncompromising radical core of what used to be called gay liberation. "We know who Sylvia Rivera is, don't we?" Roar! "We know who Marsha P. Johnson is, don't we?" Roar! We know who Miss Major, our living legend, is, don't we?" Roar again. The agenda comes out of their lives, their actions: on mass incarceration, police violence, the violence of men, the dangers of illegal sex work, on homelessness, on health care. They were street queens. They couldn't take cover in passing, in fitting in, so they went the other way, the goddess route, the stuff of legends. You told me how you tired of it, of how it exhausted you to be Venus. You didn't want to be fabulous anymore. You wanted the right to be ordinary.

Raquel takes aim closer to home, lambasting white-led and queer-led nonprofits, ornamenting themselves with Black trans people but whose core agenda is elsewhere. And worse, tell Black trans people "that you are not worthy to be a leader of these organizations that these white folks are gatekeeping, and these resources they still gatekeep."

There's a very discreet cop presence. Cops know they've not winning the hearts-and-minds thing here. Repressive power requires consent. Here in Brooklyn, these last few weeks of the uprising for Black lives, enough people just said—*fuck that*. The more the cops rampaged, the more people just refused to be policed, until the city gave in and lifted the curfew.

Now it's all police "reform" noise again. The repeated failure of police to be anything but an unequal distributor of violence just gets them more money—because that violence is their actual function. The revolution to make a world in which you could *just be* is both practical, immediate, material—and deeply utopian.

◆

I'm remembering our impromptu seminars, in back of the club, in the rave chillout. We spoke of *intersectionality*. Multiply the lines of oppression by each other and in the square where they nearly all intersect is you—the Black trans woman. We spoke of *assemblage*, where there's no lines, just groups with indefinable boundaries, one of which gathers loosely here, under these labels but not reducible to them. We tried to think it as a *dialectic*, where the experience of those whose oppression is most specific, most particular, are also those who lead back to the totality of racialized capitalism. We spoke of the falling away from a Platonic ideal of Woman, of the whiteness of that ideal. The Karens who are its guardians. In and against which the tactic of Black beauty, not approximating but exceeding it.

All those paths in thought led us to abolition.

I'm thinking about the wearing of white. Perhaps it refers to the Silent Parade, against lynching, a hundred years ago. The children wore white. Something about Blackness mobilizing whiteness on its own behalf. That liberation will most likely pass through an inversion of a hierarchy of values, that Platonic order of proximity to the ideal, those order-words, that it might abolish it all along with the forms of coercion that hold them in place.

We leave the amphitheater, this pride in white, walk to the park, in the sun, in the green. We don't have pride, like it was a thing you could buy; we become a pride, a collective noun. No statues topple. Some days there's no need. We sculpt the landscape for ourselves today, honor your icons and legends as ours. For someone like me, that means bearing witness to your witnessing. There's another time that connects past to present. The time that calls, and is heard calling, for the abolition of all that would not let you be.

When I say "we," that is still more symbolic than actual, intending to extend beyond this alabaster pelt of people, but barely. A solidarity beyond our various identities but falling short of a universalizing gesture. As you never stopped reminding me: I always got to go home to my safe white life.

It would be too easy for me to stick to my own hurt feelings about how often I'm excluded from womanhood. I have to deal more urgently with the question of what's called for when one becomes a white woman, a Karen. Even one who nurses to her fresh-grown breast her difference.

Venus, I can't write what you'd write here. I know my words are compromised. What does solidarity look like without sameness? When Ceyenne speaks, when Raquel speaks, when you spoke of certain things to me, I can't say: I feel your pain. All I can say is: I feel my own pain when you speak of yours. When I witness the joy of Black trans women, I can't say: I feel your joy. All I can say is: you open for me the feeling of another joy. The strategy and tactics of aligning our struggles is politics. The sculpting of situations that might bind us is art. An art you never got to make.

3.3

(To Cybele)

You've had many names, Cybele. That one you got by chance. I call you that because of all your names it's the one I find most pretty. It's not your secret name. That's not for all to know.

I've never written to a god before, Cybele, let alone the one who to the Greeks and Romans was the mother of all gods. It's not a thing an atheist usually does. As an atheist, I might live without you, but somehow, you're still there. You gods just refuse to die. You're always around, undead, in the phantasmagoria of everyday life. You're forever being invoked and involved.

It's those who have the least that need gods the most. When a people have nothing, we can still have a god. When nobody will help us, comfort us, fight for us, there's still the gods. This is tricky. There's the gods of power and the gods of the people. Their gods and our gods—and they're usually aspects of the same gods. Faith is folk fentanyl, but also the callus of a callous world.

Like in Jean Genet's *The Balcony*, with the republic on fire, the ruling class sparks up holograms of the most terrifying versions of the reigning gods. Around here it's the most domineering dickhead sort of sky-god, the god of order and punishment. The one who doesn't play well with others. I suppose it's to be expected, now that the republic is dying, that its most violent god would be emboldened to demand yet more sacrifices. The decaying rituals of this flailing state seem more wretched every year.

The thrall of god as order and order as god. Here in New York, the votaries of this order hang around street corners, in

subway stations, devoted to the rosaries of their phones, in their robes of blue, stroking the butts of their guns. Every year, the city pays for more of them from our communal offerings. Spleen of a splenetic world.

There's plenty of order-worshippers attracted to your cult too, Cybele, great mother that you are. They call you Nature. I wonder though if they honor you the way you crave. They make you an earth mother and use your nature as the alibi to declare girls like me unclean. This earth cult of order aligns itself so readily with the sky cult of order. It's all about order to them, regardless of whether order comes from below or above, from earth or eternity, mommy or daddy.

Gods are always all the things we say they are, even if they are contradictory: order and chaos, sameness and difference, death and creation. I just want other ways of saying your name, other rites that might entreat you. Cybele: goddess of thresholds, transitions, of the mountain and the city, of the deep, dark, silent caves and of the noisiest street rave. It won't surprise you, or anyone, that it's your messy, joyful, open, weirdo energy that I honor. Even if it isn't all of you.

You came from the east, from Phrygia, and were always something exotic, other, troubling to the Greek or Roman sensibility. Nonetheless, they used you for their intrigues and colonial projects as they pleased. They tried to tame you. Yet there you sat with a lion in your lap. The lion answers to you, and you, to nobody. Power wants to claim you, use you, but those cats bite.

To the Greeks, you were a bit of an underground sensation. Popular on the margins, with outsiders and with citizens who felt outsider-like. They robed themselves in your otherness and embroidered on it. Made you one of their rave gods. Singing and dancing and getting high as fuck. The Greeks put that tambourine in your hand. All the same to you: gods are protean. Take whatever work you can get.

It's what came with you that was trouble. They wanted you, Cybele, but not Attis, your lover, and what Attis might signify.

They had to change the myth of Attis so they wouldn't have to change their world. They changed the sequence of your myth to suit the ruling order.

The one thing their version of the Cybele and Attis myth have right is that this love cut deep. The Attis you loved was a mere shepherd, an ordinary worker, not some grand prince or king. Ordinary, but also not. Your love was for neither a man nor a woman, as they understand those things. In the language of my time, Attis was trans, a t-girl, a tall girl, a girl like us. It's a scandal, as we're not supposed to be loved—just fucked.

You loved Attis, and your love didn't waver. Attis loved you too, but not so well. She could not love herself. Attis, from the start, is what we'd now call trans, and you knew that, and loved her anyway. She just couldn't believe in your love, Cybele. I know that feeling. Many of us do. When I transitioned, I thought I'd never be loved again.

Not believing in your love, Attis went off and fucked some other girl. Trust me, hun, it meant nothing. But it made you so terribly sad. The thunder and the floods, the fires and the gales. It's your pain and rage. Which is why we party so hard for you. As if it might cheer you up. As if it might put you in your balmy, breezy mood.

The one constant in the stories is the part that's right: Attis takes up a sharp implement and cuts away her testicles. It's the sequence that got altered. Changed from a story about offering to a story about ordering. Attis does not de-nut out of penance for having left you for another. She did it long before. It's how the story starts. She cut and offered them to you. It's how you met. It's two gestures: the cut, for herself; the gift, for you. Not a sacrifice; Attis feels well rid. Attis remakes her body and honors you as the goddess of the power to remake the world.

Girls like us need no explanation for the cut of Attis. She's just a t-girl crafting flesh. But the ancients were nuts about castration (like some today). They needed a story to explain why a freeborn "man" would do that. Unlike the moderns, they knew firsthand what happened if you cut the balls off a goat, ram, bull or horse—or a slave. Knew more than Freud at least, who was clueless about what bit got cut. But they could only think it as a taking-away, a loss, a fall.

There's so many of their myths where the cut balls give rise to monsters. As if that could only be a bad thing. You and girls like me, Cybele, we love monsters. They're modern. They demonstrate the ways the world could become otherwise. They're the sign of fresh things. This is your world in all the ways it comes and cums.

This is what they never understand about you, and girls like us. If you are the goddess of creation, why take the t-girl Attis as a lover? Because creation is not just procreation. You are the goddess of all makings and doings. Of all the ways differences enters the world. Of all the ways the world edits and arranges its elements. Goddess of praxis. That's why Attis offers her cut flesh to you. For love of the world.

In your mountain home, you surround yourself with lions, and sometimes wolves, but also with working people, with shepherds, hunters, foragers, blacksmiths, beekeepers. They dance for you, they dance with you, follow the lines you lay. They curve them, queer them, twist with you a living, healing, and home. All with a careful step, never forgetting that your lions kill at will.

Your making isn't pure. There's always a little art, a little technics. Something girls like us know well. If you'll pardon the anachronism: you have always had a special relation to us t-girls. With those who honor you as mother and who are ourselves capable of mothering but always and only in ways made otherwise.

◆

Content warning for any trans women reading this: I speak about us, but it's an us that's only ever some of us. Us is another. To those who don't want to be included: there's plenty of other covens of care. Maybe we can federate our various packs and prides without needing borders round us.

To give us our ancient name: we are the Galli, the celebrants of Cybele. Maybe it means those who drank from the river Gallus, in Phrygia, your home. They think its waters make us mad, but to us it brings us to our senses. And we are nothing if not sensual when we grace you. Maybe "Galli" comes from "Galatians," Celtic people who'd moved into Phrygia by the time the Romans took an interest in your cult. The Romans thought the Celts were fags.

By the time the Romans came around, we had a look and could carry. We wore robes of mauve and saffron, sprinkled in trinkets, hair bleached and braided long, perfumed with myrrh. Tall caps instead of crowns, our makeup bright and vulgar, icons strung about our breasts. We danced to wild music, to drums and cymbals, tambourines and double flutes. We sashayed down the main drag. On our feast day, even the Romans threw roses at our feet, because every t-girl deserves her roses while she lives.

The Romans gawked and cheered, but only when we made a spectacle of ourselves. We were too much for those uptight breeders. Even Catullus blanched at the sight of us. He understood the want, at least, to be outside masculinity, even if we freaked him out. The rest of those Roman scriptwriters just used us as material. They made us the domesticated other that could be safely internal to their self-same selves. Like house cats.

Rome, in its day: it was Hollywood and the Pentagon, all in one. All spectacle and violence. They bought out any cult they thought would be good for morale. You were recruited in the war against the African Hannibal. You probably didn't help them win, but we let them believe you did.

Did your sacred stone come with you to Rome? The ancient sources are unclear. It's been lost, but it's still in the world, somewhere. It's so fitting that it's a black meteorite—alien thing from far beyond the horizon. Goddess of both bright earth and blank otherness.

They wanted you, but not the Galli, not me and my transsexual sisters. We came as part of a package deal. Those Roman hacks who wrote about us couldn't decide if we were a joke or a threat. The Galli, t-girls, we're just the score, the cut, where the otherness appears. The mark at which the fanatics of the order of earth and of the order of the sky pale and seethe. An otherness both alien and most intimate—right here in the flesh.

When the Romans acquired the IP to your cult, Cybele, they tried to fete you their way: killing rams and bulls, padding about in puddled blood. Then they'd go off to watch sports. That's Romans for you. I sometimes think their slave state never ended. We Galli became part of their spectacle, for them to gawk at in the street. It's a living.

Then came the Christian sky-god cult, who just flat-out hated us. Their idea of the sacred is flesh-hating misery. That's not for us. We don't like sacrifice. We're now. We dance with chants, with ululation. Even cut our own flesh to feel the thrill of chosen pain. We go into flesh, into this wounded life, and through its nerve, merge with worlds.

Personally, I'm not here for the cutting, but I do take pleasure from the pain of a tattoo in a sensitive spot or two. The first time I ever called your name, Cybele: I lay face down on the table, while our sister Larch Needles carved her pretty, twisty lines on the back of my left thigh. A freehand pattern she drew, sourced from cracked ice on the nearby Hudson River.

It's not really my thing, but I've relished the thwap and sting of a riding crop on that same thigh. Dahlia, before she turned professional, used to come by and thrash me. For her own amusement—she wasn't into me. My pain threshold for a stroke of the crop from Dahlia was a seven out of ten. Getting inked by Larch Needles took it to eleven—for three hours. I called your name. In vain, I knew. Yet still the calling helped.

There's no bargaining with you. The pain, the plagues, that's all you too. There's not much here for us mortals but the passing show of life. Your girls know a thing or two about that.

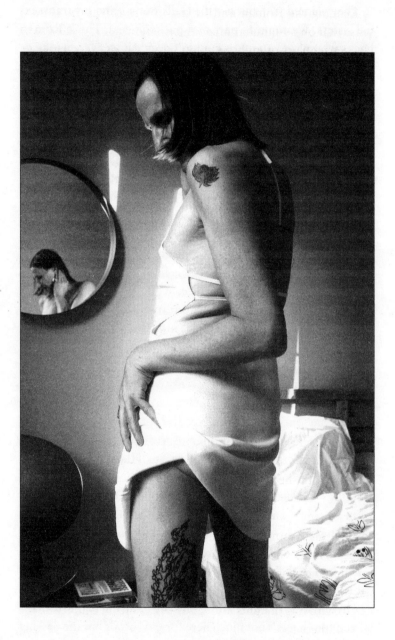

Reading the Roman and Christian writers on the Galli, I sense that oh-so-familiar mix of fascination and revulsion. The classics scholars of my time aren't much better. I read between the lines. We modern t-girls know from the other side what they see, or think they see—and see a fuller life.

The Galli drinking pregnant horse piss to keep that skin smooth—and grow tits. The Galli making coin for the temple selling ass to those Roman pricks. The t-girl loving Galli's T4T sex and feelings and trans dyke drama. Or liaisons on the down-low with respectable citizens, never to be acknowledged in public. For whom sometimes our asses are the threshold to your threshold.

Like that time I hooked up with Jane. Met on a dating app. Drinks and confessions. It's remarkable what people tell girls like us. Back to her hotel. I'm working, with tongue and fingers, on cunt and clit. She starts to cry. I hold her. Nobody has touched her like that in a while, but its more that nobody had heard her story. What she'd said over drinks. That sometimes there's someone else. There's Jane, and there is David.

"Are you David now?"

"Yes."

"Would he like to cum?"

"Yes."

So I lubed my fingers in his juices and fucked his ass with them. And he came and cried all at once. Then I held him for a spell. Until she sweetly bid me leave.

◆

When I read about you and us, what I read between the lines most of all is Galli mothering fresh girls into existence, into the life. And doing so in ritual garments. Not depending on cis doctors in their hospital gowns. I see our covens of care, no doubt with lots of fights and feuds—that side of our brittle life was all there too.

We had our special days in Rome, to be seen, and then

pushed aside again. Like Pride Month in New York. The Galli putting on a good drag show, so that the Romans could alleviate their gender panic at a safe remove. Not much has changed. A handful of spectacular t-girls are allowed to flit around the bright edges of the culture industry. Or, like me, academia. That token visibility does nothing for the rest.

Might have thought Lucretius would have understood. He gets that you are more poem than thing, an endless, self-creating, self-varying, self-elaborating beat. Verse-world, made of letters, smallest flecks there are, endlessly combinable. He just doesn't get that there's many ways a world, or poem, can be born. That it's not all cock-in-cunt cis-het sex through which you make what's made.

Nor does Lucretius get that we Galli are sacred because we're the mark of another making. A body can be otherwise. It's a surprisingly ancient thing, that bodies can be modern, flesh made and remade fresh. And yet: with transsexual wit, our sister Luce deLire reads Lucretius as one of us: the poem of Lucretius has a cut, right where it talks about the Galli. Something is absent, offered to you, perchance. A hole made in a poem; a poem made whole by a cut.

For us moderns, the world isn't a poem. It's some more problematic form. The world is autofiction, lol.

The loveliest thing in Lucretius is that you gods are real but are indifferent to human stuff. Our actions bring neither help nor harm. Lovely, but for us girls also dangerous. In ancient times, plenty of Romans were convinced we had access to your goddess power. That we could tell of the future. That our curses worked. We're still other, forever on the fringe of public life, but now when our sisters are kicked to the curb it is not as sacred wolves and lions, but only as something profane, as feral cats and stray dogs.

Those around here who think they own God say their sky god wants us girls dead. The earth-mother crones concur. Among those around here who don't believe in gods, who weirdly believe in the secular as if it too wasn't godlike, they think we're harmless, good for diversity, equity, and inclusion brownie points. Yet that dispensation can be withdrawn when inconvenient in affairs of city and state.

Perhaps reclaiming our sacred power could just be a matter of good tactics. We used to curse; now we cancel—and it never works.

We're just a few fey creatures, but the cis-hets panic easily. Imagine the horror they might feel if beyond what they saw of us, they caught a glimpse of you. We are just the decoration to your most radical concept. That your powers of creation go beyond mere procreation, and—more challenging still—that your powers of destruction go beyond mere death. The end of the human, even the end of all life on earth, would be just the flick of a claw.

The Cybelocene ...

And then the part we play: that there could be femme forms that have nothing to do with procreation. That do not owe their existence to birth and suck (although it's been known for t-girl tit to give out milk). The avatar of which can only be—us. The Galli. We who drank from the druggy river that bade us shed a manhood we felt as madness.

◆

It's been hard for me to love this world, as it is. It's been hard for me to love this body, as it is. For the longest time I could only think of how things ought to be. To the love of this world, of this body, as it is, I give your name, Cybele. World and flesh can be made otherwise, with a little art and science, with a lot of collective will. The making starts with the "as it is." A praxis of what can be, rather than of what ought.

The more dogmatically secular someone is, the more they are likely hooked on some god they can't even name. You gods are all so cunning. You change your names, your attributes. You even take the form of seemingly secular abstractions. I found some sky god hiding in my desire to deny this world in favor of an ideal one. I found some sky god hiding in my belief that changing my flesh would be too literal minded, that I could just be a queer free spirit.

I no longer invoke those gods. I turn to you instead. Not that I think you can hear me or ever answer. I write my prayer toward your vast indifference. I'm not expecting you'll review it.

Even your absence has its uses. What is other to me need not be some other mere human that I mark myself against in subtweeted snark. Praxis, if it's to be collective, needs a third between each you-and-me. Especially when it's femmes you want to organize. So that we need not always be rivals. We're such lupine bitches.

I used to call that thirdness communism. It was always far away, never here but to come. Immanent or imminent, but not actual, not now. Neither earth mother nor sky god, just a horizon. An order-word all the same.

Instead, I'll call the thirdness by your name, Cybele, or one I fished from a meme, from that most labile stream of creation that is language: femmunism. A name for what's both apart from each of us and a part of each of us, for what's here and now and actual and shared.

When I call your name, Cybele, the calling, it's not to you— it's to us.

Postscript

4.1

(To McKenzie)

Do you remember when you saw Prince that time, at the Sydney Cricket Ground? The Diamonds and Pearls Tour, in 1992. A dismal night. Your last with Edward. It was raining. A cooler night than you'd expected. And yet Prince fired up the stage with that art which is a sound, a feeling, and a gesture all at once. Reminiscent of Little Richard in its everything. Music as a passage of the body through its animal want and human hurt. This crying-out flesh, this funk, this blues. Through memory of moments when a thought, a feeling, a sensation ventured through the air in a pretty arc, maybe we can get through moments where none of that seems possible.

Have I caught you at a bad time? I know I have. I wrote to you at age twenty and got no reply. I'm trying again now you're forty. That's usually the notch in time when all the paths that seemed fresh a score of years before become the ruts of habit. It seems a common thing to be unhappy in one's forties. You avoided that by reinventing your life. Fell in love with Christen, got married, emigrated. Started your career all over in America. You thought you had the energy, the strength, the will, to change your life. And now you've found out maybe you don't. You seem fragile to yourself now, and vulnerable to the world.

I chose to write to you while you are on another visit to Newcastle, our hometown, this time after long flights, from New York to Los Angeles to Sydney, and then the train up the coast to Newcastle. The view from the carriage of those sand-stone bluffs, the gray-green leaves, and especially the blood-red waratahs on their long stems—a landscape whose loss pains me still. I have a tattoo of a waratah now.

You finally got some rest in your hotel room. There's a view of Newcastle Hospital out the window, or at least the buildings. It's condos now. Below it, Newcastle Beach, where you and your big sister used to come in the summertime when you were little. This hotel room might even be the same one you shared with Christen, that time you brought her home to meet your family. On the first morning you drew back the curtains to look at the beach and there were dolphins playing in the surf. Her open delight, and how you loved her for it.

This time, you came home for your father's funeral. And now that's done, but there'll be no quick trip home. I'll come to the extraordinary circumstances of this delay. They rather overshadow all your other feelings about being home, or what was home. It makes you think of that song by the Triffids: "Erase my name from your lips as we kiss."

Your older siblings had to manage your father's decline. You were far away. You were always, will always be, the youngest. The little brother; the little sister. Well, not yet. That's to come. You chose to channel the possibilities of your life in several directions and put a few other things ahead of becoming a girl. Who's to say that was a good or bad call? The thing one starts to feel around forty, which I know for certain around sixty, is that there's only so many moves you get to make, but you can still make plenty.

Even now I'm avoiding how you feel about Ross when he passed. You were spared the task of making funeral arrangements but had to give the eulogy. I just found that document in my digital archive. Reading it again now, I'm struck by the warmth of it. A tone governed by social convention, but also sincere. Our memory of him has hardened over time, and perhaps I should remember how you remembered him, before I took such distance.

Do you remember that time, back when Newcastle was still

home: there'd been storms and floods, and right after, an uncannily bright day? You'd come down to the beach and there were watermelons floating in the water, washed down from farms upriver. Those green heads bobbing in the surf. Bursting open, pink flesh in the foam. The Hunter River just keeps flowing, fast or slow, but always flowing into the harbor, out to sea, carrying us all along. With your parents gone, you and your siblings are now the old heads in the family, probably next to be borne along to old ocean.

Like most people you're making your own family to try to dam up time. You fell in love. You married. You're trying to make a home, far away from here, in New York. You wonder if it was all a mistake.

It all happened so quickly. Only a year or so ago you were giving away your Sydney possessions to a group of refugees. They welcomed all your kitchen stuff but were puzzled by your audiophile turntable. You told them to sell it for no less than three hundred.

Compared to them your emigration was an easy one. The Australian dollar was only worth about sixty American cents, but at least worth something. Christen had found an apartment, on Frost Street in Williamsburg. You had a job waiting for you. A one-year visiting appointment in comparative literature at Binghamton University.

The commute to Binghamton is four hours, on the bus. To that rat-infested apartment by the Chenango River. Your roommate departed after the shooting, even though it was on the other end of Front Street. Money is tight, paying rent in two places and supporting both Christen and yourself. The conventions of American higher education are and will remain a mystery. Your degrees are from places unknown. Your references are from people unknown. It's unclear if there's a job for you anywhere when this Binghamton one ends. You are and will remain an outsider.

◆

All that is now cast into uncertainty anyway. Here in Newcastle, just after the funeral, you were walking around the David Jones department store. They sell fresh-baked cookies there, or biscuits as you would still say, and that aroma always made us happy. Maybe our mother brought us here? The details aren't clear, but there's something warm around the absent memory, and you've come to savor it. People are looking at you strangely. Maybe it's the New York Yankees baseball cap, marking you as an outsider here too now.

In the coffee shop nearby, the television is on with the sound up, and it's not showing sports. Evil-twin jet planes javelin into their tower twins in downtown New York, over and over, video replay cut with live video from the scene and of talking heads. A modern nightmare. You watch with the others, open mouthed. Nobody takes your coffee order.

It happened late the previous night, Newcastle time. Hours ago, and you knew nothing of it. Absorbed in the choppy wake of the funeral. Forget coffee. You hurry back to your father's former apartment, television on, trying without success to call Christen. The lines are down. You call the few people you know in New York. No connection. The need for coffee makes its insistent plea and you drink that instant shit that your father favored. The phone rings. It's a friend of a friend in Iowa with the news that a friend of a friend in New York can report that Christen is safe and at a friend's place. You try calling there.

The news unfolds like a weird global media event. These were the subject of your first book, *Virtual Geography*. The way the electric vectors of money, information and violence create their own space-time. The way the flow of news is one of the weapons in the information war. But also: the way that the irruption of the weird global media event defamiliarizes meaning, opening a break in ruling fictions, but only for a moment, before that's all cut out by "expert" talking heads, smooth montages with authoritative narratives. Attending to the moment of the event is a method for reading the underlying form of information at work as power.

You don't feel much like taking notes this time. This lurching dread is the other side of that modern feeling of vertigo, one that you've often embraced from the safety of having places and people to call home. It's not hard to predict what's coming. Nationalism, militarism, probably war. The Futurists weren't kidding when they called war the "world's only hygiene." There'll be fascists again, or something like them. What they want to sterilize is everything and everyone you know and love. They want to be at war with the world.

It would have been a welcome extra few days at your sister's place in the country if the situation had been different. Trying to call home, which now means Christen in Williamsburg. Fruitless calls to the airline. Nights in your sister's spare room, with a shelf of your mother's books. Reading a Penguin paperback of F. Scott Fitzgerald, which you'll take home without asking.

◆

So here you are, at two-score years, your energy levels already a little dimmed, confronting a concatenating turning point in your life. The death of your father, the struggle to make a go of it in your new married life in New York, and all in a moment of geopolitical crisis.

It'll all work out, after a fashion.

You've lost confidence in yourself. It's a thing that happens around two-score years. What I know after three score is that even if one has less energy and has already narrowed what might still potentially be the final cut of life through the diversions one hazards and can't undo—there's knowledge and wit enough distilled into the flesh to push on through. Play your Prince CD, the one you brought in the round orange pod of a case, and remember when you saw him perform and how that moment felt. It's all there in the body, the means to think and

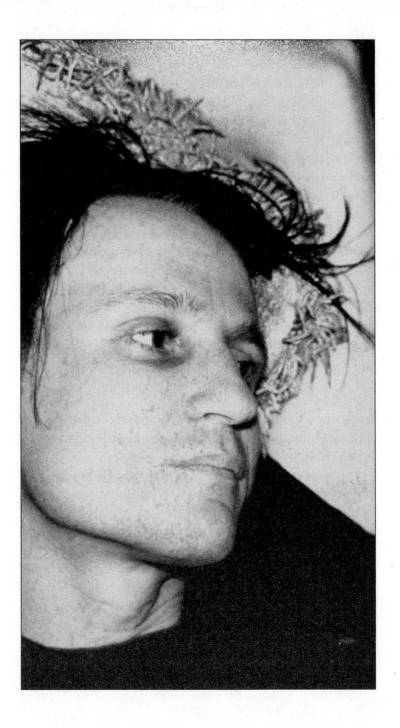

feel and work and play and place and dance through even the tricky chord changes.

It's tempting to try and become the sort of writer the conventions of American scholarship demand, and maybe there's another timeline where that's what you chose to do. Who knows? Maybe you have a better career in that one. Maybe in that one you're in some snowy college town as the [Insert Name of Rich Doner Here] Chair of Media Studies at [Insert Name of Slave Profiteer Here] University. That's not how it worked out, in this timeline at least. Maybe there's others where your life is worse. Who's to say this is the only reality?

Without really thinking about it, without conscious calculation, you'll just write what you feel compelled to write. In and against the cursed language of our times. Since you don't do well with being mentored, maybe it has to be that way. If I can tell you one thing, it's that your art will pull you through, although not without imposing its conditions.

Your writing isn't good yet. I won't say it gets great, but it at least gets better. Is getting better. A piece of the writing that from my vantage point is your break already exists: the early versions of *A Hacker Manifesto*. What possessed you to write it? Serious question, as I really don't know anymore. I read it now as if it's by someone else. I is an-other.

I suppose it came organically out of the time you put into the avant-garde of coders, artists, theorists and activists who played with the internet before anyone knew how to make it a business. There's that Marxism that only sees residual media and cultural forms as resistant to commodification, whether low (Pasolini) or high (Adorno). Your hunch was that there'd be possibilities on the forward edge of forces of communication and culture, and you weren't alone in that. There really was an avant-garde of emergent forms. Like all avant-gardes— we lost.

It's a good instinct, though, to look for the avant-gardes of forms for mediated life that were momentarily one step ahead of the meat grinder and brain blender of work and money. Follow the creators of possible forms, practices, moods, languages. In the milieu between militants, bohemians and the avant-garde—that's your sort. Maybe even your class.

For this writing to come, you'll spend a long time finding genres, those conventions that form readers' expectations. It will turn out that finding genre (text) is not unconnected to finding gender (flesh). It will take a long time to work that out. Your own body will be one of your later books, written in flesh-speak, the needle a stylus marking your blood with bioidentical estrogen.

An early hint: it will take years for *A Hacker Manifesto* to come out, I'm sorry to say. It will be rejected often. But when it does, it will be a small, elegantly designed hardback. You'll give it to a colleague you had up till then respected, who will dismiss it as a "handbag book." Which will secretly tickle you as an unintended compliment. You imagine your reader carrying it in her handbag to read on the subway, or waiting in line at the drug store, or at the bar waiting for her lover. To be read within the textures of the interstitial time of everyday life—what could be better? Change life, Rimbaud said.

Keep writing like this, where the entire form of the book, from its language through to its shape, design, not to mention how you talk about it, what events surround it, are all part of a collaborative practice of working the text into some curious corner of the world. The book and author as an event, a situation, a total work of art, but in a minor way. And it's just fine if the community it draws, or joins, is a little opaque to the larger noise.

As a scholar you are supposed to have a "field." It's a colonial mentality. Put your stakes in, claim it, "break new ground," defend it as if it was your private property. Then "pave the way" for others to suburbanize yet more. You'll be tempted to think like this, but it's not your best impulse. As a writer, you just want to pass through, leave offerings, tidy up a bit, and move on. You're a vector across institutions, fiefdoms, status hierarchies.

You won't be rewarded for that in conventional ways, but they'll keep asking you back when they get bored with themselves. It's a living. They'll let you in the back door of the ivory towers like hired help and escort you out the same way. You won't be asked to stay. Particularly after you've questioned where the ivory came from.

You're going to have some grand adventures. You're more of an artist whose medium is the book, but where the book could be anything. The book as we know it is a surprisingly modern thing, and always changing. Each book you make will twist its genre just a little, put some torque on it to tease and seduce readers' expectations. From that play with genre, eventually you'll figure out the gender game.

You were never one of those writers who presumes to write from authority. You write to make sense, to sort out. It's the essayist's praxis. Writing is a technic extruding from a body, sounding the situation of that body, by the mark. It's a visceral art, like that of Little Richard, like that of Prince, but for those who, like you, lack coordination or stage presence. You're a musician of words who can't sing a note and was too incompetent even to join a band of three-chord wonders. The first writing you were paid for was about music.

The genre of a book, of a body, is a musical art, a time-based work of improvisation upon the given. You don't have to keep playing the same old tune. You can modify the form of man, memoir, essay, woman, academic monograph. You don't have to break a form—indeed there's something coercive about that —the bad side of modernism. You can play with it instead. Play with the forms as given. Until they expand our possibilities, meet our needs.

People will ask you why you write so much. You have had a variety of evasive answers and will for a long time. Now I just say it's a mental illness. Equal parts mania, dissociation, and dysphoria. You just cultivated your weird brain's limitations so you could do fairly well-paid wage labor with it. With luck and love and money, that's probably within the reach of most weird-brain people—and most people have weird brains. The good life will be when everyone can live well with and from what makes us different.

Someone once asked Charlie Parker what his religion was, and he said: "I am a devout musician." It's a modern faith. Praxis as open-ended gestures gathering and swarming into form. Somehow it just calls for respect, for reverence, for celebration, for honoring, when artists embroider on the conventions of their world and make it fresh, particularly when they overcome antiblackness too.

I know you found your first year in America hard, but it's not something you get to complain about. A middle-class white person, apparently a man, with a legit visa, who loves and is loved, has a job and stable housing. It's a matter of taking advantage of those resources. Classic case of the ambitious provincial outsider come to the big city. It's a decadent age, and in America cultural capital is hoarded by those who think it their rightful inheritance. You'll meet plenty of successful writers and academics whose parents were successful writers and academics. And plenty of artists whose parents were collectors. They're often a bit bored—and boring. That's your in.

But don't imagine they'll let you join the club. Your people are outside that world. You're Lucien in Balzac's *Lost Illusions*. Just try not to have Lucien's fatal flaw, that desire for conventional prestige. It's more fun among the queers and chorines anyway. Besides, you don't have the pedigree, the breeding, or the training. Your French is weak. You're a better writer than scholar.

You'll get to be what you really wanted, strolling about a great city in its overripe era. You won't have masses of readers, but you'll have enough. Interesting ones, and various, over the years. You'll do fine. When you sell out, get a good price—and close-read the contracts.

Your provincial petit bourgeois background can make you cynical. There'll be mouths to feed: four humans and two cats. And if you're not careful, you'll become more hack than hacker. You can't afford aristocratic airs, aloof from business matters; nor can you afford to let on in your dealings that you need the money.

Your writing will be interesting when the meat of it touches a little mystery. It will come to you late, but something hovering on the edge of awareness is the surface tension of the numinous. You're not and never will be religious. But a problem you'll put off, and even longer than transition, is a language for that unseen pooling beyond what's known. Some call it Cthulhu or The Real like it's some great other to their suburban souls, but unboundedness doesn't spook you.

Maybe not everything needs to be known. Maybe things unknown don't have to be imagined as threats or brought under control. Maybe we could just touch the outer surface of the unknown and not need to penetrate its mysteries, to fuck it. Maybe the gods would rather we leave them alone.

◆

But you are afraid of something. Afraid of becoming someone else. Of writing with the flesh directly. You've felt what's possible. Found a little trick.

When you got to your hotel room in Newcastle, exhausted from a night and day of traveling, you still found time for your little ritual. Dim the lights. Put on some music. Lay out your black garter belt, your black stockings, that padded bra you stole from Christen, also black. Put the ensemble on, one piece at a time, fingers trembling. Admire yourself in the full-length mirror. At least your thighs are nice.

It's all clichés, this slutty bedroom wear, and you know it. That's why it works. To shock flesh into awareness. The contrast

of black nylons on white flesh. It's a ritual to invoke another body for another self. Hello, Karen.

The moment in between is precious, and more interesting than the metamorphosis. That sideways time where signs swim on surfaces of skin and start to rearrange. The signs don't matter. They're conventions. It's the molten core they draw toward them that's of interest. What feels both agreeably sexed and queerly sexual.

Your map of the terrain of genders is still crude. One doesn't learn that much about femininity when you're just a tourist in it. What if you left that other home you hate yet got so comfy in—your masculinity? A much-delayed departure. It gaslights you into staying: it's too late, you'll never be a woman, you'll be a brick, you'll be alone and unloved and, almost as bad in your mind, unread.

Leaving masculinity, leaving Ken behind, that will take a long time. Now it's done. It's a very different feeling, being a transsexual woman in the world, every day, every night. Hardly euphoric. Rather ordinary. My sexuality lost that tingling charge that cross-dressing gives you, but there's other pleasures. And you'll be loved. Turns out there's a few rare humans in the world, trans or not, for whom a little gender weirdness is not repulsive or a thrilling fetish but just their everyday experience too.

And you'll write. You'll learn to write again. It won't come easily. Those abandoned docs you'll pass from hard drive to hard drive, the ones Karen wrote, the ones that never take off and fill out, that won't be for nothing. The failures of the text await a reshaped flesh.

It'll take twenty years, but some day you'll be a woman in the world. She's old now, but much happier. A body at home to itself. You'll have more energy at sixty than you do now at forty.

Your life as a woman will be brief. She'll die young. That's the trade-off with late transition. These days the younger girls envy my wealth and security, and I of course envy their youth. But then some of them will have short lives too. In this world, nobody gets off without some mark upon them from transsexuality.

Come out, Karen. You won't be Karen anymore. You'll disappear. Maybe that's who's resisting. I know you're in there, Karen. Come out into the world. You can't live there, but McKenzie can, when she subsumes some of you into the new self she can bolt together once she strips you and Ken for parts to make her.

Sure, the first year or two will be rough. Your marriage will end, although for a lot of reasons. There will be much random crying. You hate that there seems to be a sheet of opaque glass between your subjectivity and your emotions. Once you're on estrogen there'll be no separation at all for a while and you'll just plunge right to the bottom of feeling. You'll learn how to swim.

Your early outfits will be tragic as fuck. But you'll figure out what looks good on you, like any woman does. No hips to speak of and tiny tits but nice shoulders and thighs. You can quit worrying about your skinny crip calves. It's a bit embarrassing when cis women give you their wardrobe cast-offs, but you'll be grateful for the black Prada sleeveless dress borrowed from a Lacanian analyst. Well, "borrowed," sure. She's not getting it back. She's one of the good ones, but the Lacanians are not our friends. Psychoanalysis owes us reparations for a century of harm.

I suppose then it's four things weighing on you right now, and there's nothing I can do about it. All of them are kinds of *expatriation*. From dad, from nation, from masculinity itself, and in a moment when the militarized fatherland is ramping up its power.

◆

Twenty years into your future, I'll return to Australia as a woman, for the first time. I'll not go to Newcastle. We have no ties there anymore. I'll get a fancy hotel room in Sydney with sparkling views of the harbor. It's a flying visit. I have to go back and teach. The room is not ready when I arrive, so I go to the Botanic Garden. Colors, scents, and sounds, all so familiar even after a long absence, making me cry.

There'll be dinner with all our Australian family later but first lunch with our sister in the hotel lounge. Two rounds of gin and tonics. She says she always wanted a sister and now she has one. We both cry, then dry our tears, and move on—like the WASPs we are.

The conventional transsexual memoir used to end with transition, with becoming a woman. Sorted. As if that made a self finally whole and complete. But we've never believed in wholeness, or the self, or completion. I is an-other. (Which is perhaps the formula of femininity.) Life got better, but there's no happy ending. Just one situation after another. We lost faith in historical necessity. This is another sort of memoir, or maybe no sort at all.

Thrumming between two lives, fresh life needs another past as well as a new present, and the past comes after the present. I came out, but not as the culmination of a narrative progression, with a beginning, middle, and end. It just happened, and I make the past make sense of it after the fact. I suspect it's always like that. But then, we never trusted stories. They've let us down so many times.

The best I can do is write these letters, to paper over the past that's lost.

4.2

Attachments

The first letter to McKenzie, and the form for this whole book, came out of a workshop on the epistolary at the Poetry Project run by Kay Gabriel. This book is in dialogue with various other trans writers, and I learned a lot from other epistolary trans books, by Kay, Cecilia Gentili, Hazel Jane Plante and Akwaeke Emezi. The Rimbaud line is a *détournement*, copied and modified, from two of his letters, which appear as a preface in the New Directions edition of *Illuminations*. There are other *détourned* lines form other authors scattered throughout the book. If you find one, it's a little gift to your literary knowledge, no need to @ me about it. There are several versions of the Little Richard in Newcastle story, on which see Roland Bannister in *Hunter Living Histories*, May 6, 2019.

The first part of the first letter to Joyce appeared in the *Sydney Review of Books* and is included in an anthology of writing from it. The second part derives from my contribution to a panel for the exhibition "The Clamor of Ornament" at The Drawing Center, engages with writing by Shola von Reinhold and Juliana Huxtable, and draws on texts I've written about their work for *e-flux journal*.

The second letter to Joyce appeared briefly online for the Sydney publication *Neighbourhood Paper*, which ceased operation shortly after. Since I was never paid, I asked for it to be "unpublished."

For the letter to Sue, my thanks to the "Lost Newcastle" group on Facebook. The distinction between mothers and mothering I owe to Sophie Lewis.

The letter to Mu borrows a couple of lines from a much-earlier piece I wrote for *Meanjin* called "Just Like a Prayer." The view of Australian multiculturalism here is from my reading of Ghassan Hage. "Song to the Siren" is by Tim Buckley, but my friends and I knew it from the version by This Mortal Coil.

The letter to Christen interpolates lines from Harron Walker and Diana Goetsch, and from songs by Elysia Crampton Chuquimia. Christen Clifford's *Interiors* project is documented at WeAreAllPinkInside.com.

Part of the letter to Jenny was written to be performed at Nowadays with music by Body Techniques in the *Writing on Raving* series created by Zoë Beery and Geoffrey Mak. A recorded version can be found on my Bandcamp page. I've incorporated a bit of Shelley's "Epipsychidion," and half a line from Ethel Cain. Thanks to Sul Mousavi for introducing me to her work. There's also lines from my friends Eva Hayward and Isobel Ward. That trans femmes might enjoy and suffer all the effects of every kind of love is recent in our art, and I'm thankful to Pet Wife, Jamie Hood, Lauren John Joseph and Macy Rodman for illuminating corners of it.

The letter to Veronica was written for, and rejected by, the T4T issue of *Transgender Studies Quarterly*, and first appeared instead in *e-flux journal*. That version has footnotes, acknowledging the various sources from which it draws. The passage on the pretty is for Jessie Rovinelli and from an essay on her work, also in in *e-flux journal*. Big love for e-flux, who made space for me to explore many of the ideas that have ended up in this and other books over the years. On the topic of T4T, this book is in dialogue with those of Casey Plett, Torrey Peters, Cat Fitzpatrick. Veronica is fictional.

Venus is based on two young trans people I have known and lost and still grieve. Their stories aren't mine to tell so I have obfuscated the details of their lives in this composite tribute. The Saidiya Hartman essay mentioned is "Venus in Two Acts," *Small Axe*, June 2008. The descriptive parts about Brooklyn

Liberation for Trans Lives appeared in *Public Seminar*. I learned a lot from participating in the year of protest and celebration that remarkable event sparked, led by Qween Jean, Joela Rivera and others, and which is documented in *Revolution Is Love: A Year of Black Trans Liberation*. I am indebted also to Black trans writers including memoirs by Toni Newman, Tenika Watson, The Lady Chablis, Janet Mock, novels by Red Jordan Arobateau, the theater of Travis Alabanza and the book of interviews with Miss Major. Eva Henderson (not to be confused with Eva Hayward) is a tattoo artist who can be found as @larch.needles on Insta. Dahlia's film work as Dahlia Doll can be found at AortaFilms.com. There's another line from Shelley, this time via its *détournement* by Scritti Politti.

The letter to Cybele owes a lot to conversations with, and writing by, five trans women: Susan Stryker, Roz Kaveney, Bishakh Som, Aurora Mattia and Luce deLire. Of the scholarship consulted I'll just mention Lynn Roller, *In Search of God the Mother*, and Philippe Borgeaud, *Mother of the Gods*. I learned a lot about the protean possibilities of myth from Kathy Acker.

The Charlie Parker line in the last letter to McKenzie is from the book *Bird Lives!* An expanded sense of expatriation I got from John Hartley. I was also thinking of how masculinity is handled in trans femme writing, by Isle McElroy and Jackie Ess, for example. The questioning of "memoir" at the very end owes a lot to how transsexuality, when it inflects gender, also inflects genre, for example, in Kai Cheng Thom, T. Fleischmann, Joss Barton and Hannah Baer. See my essay "Girls Like Us" in the *White Review* for more on that.

◆

Thanks to Akin Akinwumi, who shopped the manuscript to some commercial publishers on my behalf. Without success. I was particularly charmed by the editor for whom the epistolary form "felt distancing; even the fisting scene was a bit at a remove, when what was called for seemed to be something more visceral and embodied." Which is curious, given that then as now, this book contains no fisting scene.

Special thanks to Leo Hollis, my editor at Verso. When I finally brought the book to him, he spotted at once how to fix a structural problem. As with several of my previous books, he has gently guided me toward making better books than I ever could on my own. Thanks also to Sam Smith and Mark Martin further downstream on the production side at Verso. Thanks to Chip Wilde Clifford Wark for photo editing.

Back at the end of the eighties, I received a letter from Malcolm Imrie on the Verso letterhead. He wrote to express regard for an essay I had written on Paul Virilio and said that if I had a book to propose along those lines to "bear Verso in mind." Nobody had ever suggested I could write a book before. My first book contract, for what became *Virtual Geography*, was with Verso, as was my second contract, for a book called *Love and Money, Sex and Death*. The first happened, but not with Verso; the second didn't happen until thirty years later. I am deeply indebted to Malcolm for his faith in me.

Love and Money, Sex and Death is also deeply indebted to, and embedded in, various attachments, various homes: my Australian homes, my Queens homes, my Brooklyn homes, my trans writer and raver homes, and also to the community of current and former students.

This book is for H and P and—and their familiars.

Brooklyn, December 2022

Photo Credits

Age nineteen, chairperson of the Fourteenth Macquarie University Student Council, by Kit Kellen, p. 8.

Joyce in the 1940s, possibly before she met Ross, p. 20.

Detail of the Florida Hotel, designed by Mayo & Wark, family photo, p. 21.

Learning to walk in casts, family photo, p. 28.

Going into surgery, by author, p. 36.

As one of three kings, 1960s, family photo, p. 40.

With Sue on family vacation at the Flotilla, 1960s, probably by Ross Wark, p. 49.

Mu, 1980s, by author, p. 63.

Me and Christen, 1990s, photographer unknown, p. 69.

At Riis Beach, Pride weekend 2021, by author, p. 74.

Chilling out at the rave, 2020s, selfie, p. 79.

Jenny writing, Brooklyn 2022, by author, p. 81.

Kissing Jenny at the end of a rave at "Chernobyl," 2022, by Jessica Dunn Rovinelli, p. 90.

Reclaim Pride 2021 in the Ghost dress, by Christen Clifford, p. 105.

Basquiat's grave, Green-Wood Cemetery, by author, p. 113.